# *Tarot Cards*

## A BEGINNERS GUIDE OF TAROT CARDS: THE PSYCHIC TAROT MANUAL

**Julia Steyson**

**© 2018**

# COPYRIGHT

Tarot Cards : A Beginners Guide of Tarot Cards: The Psychic Tarot Manual

**By Julia Steyson**

Furthermore, the transmission, duplication or reproduction of any of the following work, including precise information, will be considered an illegal act, irrespective whether it is done electronically or in print. The legality extends to creating a secondary or tertiary copy of the work or a recorded copy and is only allowed with express written consent of the Publisher. All additional rights are reserved.

The information in the following pages is broadly considered to be a truthful and accurate account of facts, and as such any inattention, use or misuse of the information in question by the reader will render any resulting actions solely under their purview. There are no scenarios in which the publisher or the original author of this work can be in any fashion deemed liable for any hardship or damages that may befall them after undertaking information described herein.

Additionally, the information found on the following pages is intended for informational purposes only and should thus be considered, universal. As befitting its nature, the information presented is without assurance regarding its continued validity or interim quality. Trademarks that mentioned are done without written consent and can in no way be considered an endorsement from the trademark holder.

# FURTHER READING

Thanks for purchasing Julia Steylon's comprehensive guide on Tarot Card Reading. We recommend you also get her book on Astrology and Horoscopes.

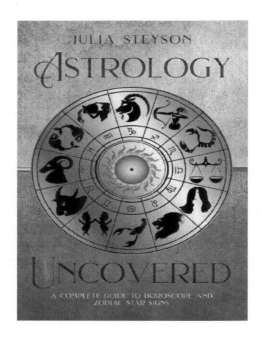

You can find it here:

https://www.amazon.com/Astrology-Uncovered-Guide-Horoscopes-Zodiac-ebook/dp/B07D6W64KZ

It is called: Astrology Uncovered: A Guide To Horoscopes And Zodiac Signs by Julia Steyson

And we also recommend you check out Julia Steyson's book on Wicca, Magic, Spells and Witchcraft. It will leave you spellbound!

It is called: Wicca Spell Book: The Ultimate Wiccan Book on Magic and Witches: A Guide to Witchcraft, Wicca and Magic in the New Age with a Divinity Code.

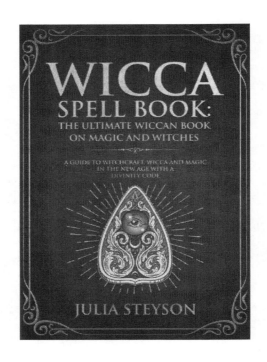

You can find it here:

https://www.amazon.com/Wicca-Spell-Book-Witchcraft-Divination-ebook/dp/B07GVLK9PZ

# TABLE OF CONTENTS

## CHAPTER THREE: THE MINOR ARCANA

**CHAPTER FOUR : HOW TO DO A TAROT
READING** ....................................................**165**

# CHAPTER ONE: GETTING STARTED

## WHAT IS TAROT?

The tarot is a deck of seventy-eight cards, which are used for divination, for gaining insight and guidance on your current situation and your path in life. All of human life, perhaps even all of life, is contained within the images of the tarot. By learning to read the cards, you will gain knowledge of yourself, of your relationships with others, and of the bigger picture, the pattern of your life. Deep symbolism and many layers of knowledge are encoded in the images of the tarot, and by learning to read the cards, you learn to delve into these layers and the many ways they reflect our human experience.

As well as giving you the individual meanings of the cards, this book will show you the ways they fit together and the stories they tell. The tarot is a picture book, illustrating human life, our responses to the world and ways of acting in it, and this book will show you how to read it. The book of the tarot works on both an outer level, showing us the events and circumstances around us, and an inner level, reflecting back to us our emotions, hopes and fears and the way they affect our actions. Tarot is a language, told in images, universal symbolism and motifs, and this book will help you to become fluent in it.

The seventy-eight cards of the tarot deck are divided into two main sections, the Major Arcana or Greater Trumps and the Minor Arcana or Lesser Trumps. The Major Arcana can be seen as a psychological or spiritual journey towards greater understanding and fulfilment, of ourselves and of the world around us. There are twenty-two 'greater trumps", taking us on a journey through the great archetypes and energies which inform our lives, from the Fool with his leap into the unknown to the completion and success of the World. The Major Arcana cards show universal forces and life experiences which we may not be able to control, but which have a profound effect on us and the way we live our lives. They include figures such as the Empress and Emperor, representing the archetypal mother and the archetypal father, and heavenly bodies such as the Sun and the Moon

The fifty-six cards of the Minor Arcana are divided into four suits, usually known as Wands, Swords, Cups and Pentacles. They are similar to the spades, hearts, diamonds and clubs of a standard deck of playing cards. Each suit is related to a particular element, symbolising, in turn, a particular area of life. Wands are the suit of fire, symbolising creativity, passion and action, and Swords are linked to the element of Air, to logic, reason and communication. Cups are the suit of water, representing our feelings and imagination, and finally, the Pentacles bring it all into manifestation in the realm of earth, symbolising the material world, our work, home and resources.

Each suit contains fourteen cards, beginning with the Ace and going up to Ten. The number cards combine symbolism from numerology with the elemental attributions of the suits to describe the realities of our journey through life, our experiences of relationships and connections with other people, the work that we do and the place that we live, all of the choices that we make on a day to day basis.

The Court cards are the Page, Knight, Queen and King, and they represent personalities and ways that we use the elemental powers in our lives. They are a kind of tarot "family" showing our progression from youth to maturity and the different ways that we experience and act in the world as we grow.

## *WHY DO WE READ THE CARDS, AND HOW DO THEY WORK?*

Most people think of tarot cards as a way of telling the future, and that is one of the ways of using the cards. But it's important to remember that we all have free will. The cards do not determine our future, our decisions and choices do that. What the tarot cards can do is help us to make those decisions, to look at possible outcomes of choices we may make, and in this way guide us on our path. The cards reflect our inner as well as our outer experience, so that they may show you your feelings around a situation, or your hopes and dreams, just as clearly as they show the situation itself.

There are many misconceptions and superstitions surrounding the tarot, and many people are put off using the cards, or even going for a reading because they fear being told that something bad will happen to them. Whilst its true that the tarot sometimes doesn't pull any punches, and may tell you what you don't want to hear, it will also tell you what you can do about it. Nothing is set in stone and even if a situation is beyond our control, we usually have some degree of choice in how we react to it. Whilst the tarot is most well known as a tool for prediction, it is actually more often used as a tool for contemplation and reflection, for connecting to our inner selves. You will find that often, you already know what the tarot cards tell you, you just didn't know that you knew!

When people say that they are scared of the tarot or of what it might tell them, their fear is more likely a fear of being exposed, of having their inner feelings and experiences brought into the open. Not only does this make many people uncomfortable, but the fact that a deck of cards, mere images printed on paper, may do so, makes them even more uncomfortable. But we might say that this discomfort also shows us tarot's greatest strength, as an objective viewpoint on our lives. The cards seemingly fall at random, and yet their meanings connect deeply to our experience and show us the "truth" of our lives, as we are experiencing it at that moment. Some believe that there is some unseen force at work around us, ensuring that the cards we pull are exactly the ones we need to see right now, others that some hidden part of our mind influences us as we shuffle and lay out the cards. There are many ideas and explanations about why the tarot works, but most come back to the idea of synchronicity, or correspondences. Most of occult (the word "occult" simply means hidden knowledge) thought is based on the idea that there is a correspondence or link between something outside of ourselves, such as the tarot cards or the planets in astrology, and something within our psyche. They do not cause or affect each other, rather they are at work in parallel, so that by looking at the external manifestation of the force, for example in the image on a tarot card, we become aware of the corresponding energy at work within us. Occultists refer to this idea using the phrase "As above, so below" - as the energies play out above us in the universe, so they also play out within us. You may have already experienced "synchronicities" when events around you seem to reflect your emotions or what is happening within you. Using the tarot is a way of consciously inviting these synchronicities, understanding them and using them to live our best lives.

## THE HISTORY AND EVOLUTION OF

## THE TAROT

The tarot cards have their origins in fifteenth-century Italy, where they developed partly as a game (giving rise also to modern day playing cards) and partly as a kind of teaching aid showing medieval religious and social images, such as Strength, Temperance and Judgement. For years they were mainly used for the game of Tarocchi and for gambling, although they were sometimes also used for fortune telling. In the eighteenth century and nineteenth centuries, occultists (those who study hidden and esoteric knowledge) became aware of the tarot cards and their powerful images, and decided that there was more to these cards than met the eye. They linked them to the hidden knowledge of ancient Egypt, to the Jewish mystical tradition of the Kabbalah, and even to traditions of ceremonial magic. Nineteenth-century occultists, especially the members of the Order of the Golden Dawn in the late nineteenth century, worked with the cards and developed them into the images that we know today. Whilst they added extra layers of meaning and correspondences to other spiritual systems such as astrology, the basic structure of the deck has changed little since the artist Bonifacio Bembo painted the first deck for a wealthy Italian family, the Viscontis, in the middle of the fifteenth century.

Many of the decks most easily available today are based on the so-called Waite-Smith deck, developed by Arthur Waite (one of those Victorian occultists mentioned above) and illustrated by Pamela Colman Smith. It was first published in 1910 and has become the basis for most tarot decks published today.

The Waite-Smith deck was the first to use images on the Minor Arcana cards. The earlier Marseilles or European tradition (still popular and widely used today) has images on the Major Arcana cards and "pips" for the Minor Arcana – seven pentacles for the seven of pentacles, three swords for the Three of Swords, and so on. Many people find that having scenes painted on all the cards, including the Minor Arcana, makes them easier to read and remember, and this is especially useful when you are first learning the cards. However the Waite Smith version of the tarot is not as definitive as some would believe, and the earlier European tradition still has much to teach us. Over time, as you become more familiar with the cards, you will find the images and tradition which work best for you. This book uses mainly the Waite Smith images, simply because they are most commonly found and referred to in the world of tarot, whilst also drawing on other traditions and versions of the tarot images.

## *CHOOSING A TAROT DECK*

When we begin to work with tarot cards, we are making a choice to work on a symbolic level, which goes deeper than using our mind and intellect. From the many hundreds of different decks available today, the right deck for you is the one whose symbolism resonates deeply for you, the one which gives you a flash of recognition as soon as you see the cards. This may not be something you can articulate or communicate with others, but as you'll soon learn, there is much about the tarot that defies easy explanation, and herein lies its power.

A wide variety of decks are available, from the traditional to the modern, with themes drawing on different belief systems and traditions and on many aspects of popular culture. Whether your interest is fairies, tattoos or Buddhism, there's a tarot deck out there to suit you. When choosing a deck, listen to your intuition and choose the one with images you are drawn to, as you will get the most profound results that way. Working with the tarot means working with symbolic energies and images, so choosing a deck with images which reflect your worldview, or maybe even challenge your worldview, is likely to bring you the best results. There's no right or wrong way to choose a deck, as long as it speaks to you on some level, and has images that resonate with your life experience and the way you see the world.

You may also want to take into account practical considerations such as the shape and size of the cards, and how easy you find shuffling them. Even something as simple as the colour palette can evoke an emotional response, and an emotional response is what you want when choosing "your" deck.

Decks can be bought online as well as in "new age" shops and bookshops. New age shops often have a folder or file with sample cards from the different decks they have available so that you can look at the cards without having to open a sealed deck. Online, there are websites such as aeclectic.net and tarotgarden.com have lists and reviews of hundreds of decks, so you can do some research before you buy to be sure of getting the deck that's right for you. Some people believe that you must be gifted a tarot deck, but there is no reliable origin for this so-called tradition, which probably dates back to when tarot decks were difficult to find and knowing somebody who had one was really the only way to obtain one. Now they are widely available, we have more opportunities to find "our" deck and make that all-important personal connection with it.

Many tarot readers end up acquiring more than one tarot deck, and some have large collections. You may find that you work regularly with one or two decks, and have others simply because you like the images. Some decks work better for quick readings, others for deep personal explorations, still others for meditation and spiritual practice.

## LOOKING AFTER YOUR CARDS

So you've got your cards, now what? The first thing to note is some easy ways to look after them, as they tend to come in a cardboard box which can get worn very quickly when you are constantly taking the cards in and out of it. Again, there are many traditions, usually of quite a modern origin, about how you should look after your cards, and again, you shouldn't worry too much about them, but follow what feels right to you. Many people believe that tarot cards should be wrapped in silk because silk is a natural fibre and is seen as a good insulator against psychic energies. So silk protects your cards on both a physical and a spiritual level. Other natural fibres such as cotton are also good, and keeping your cards in a wooden box is also a popular way to protect them. Your cards are a sacred tool and should be treated as such – look after them and they will look after you!

Many people prefer not to let others touch their tarot deck, as it can muddy the psychic energies the cards carry. Again, this is a personal preference, and of course, there is a difference between letting your nearest and dearest occasionally look through your cards, and complete strangers rifling through them.

When reading for others, many readers ask the querent (the person receiving the reading) to shuffle the decks, to add their own energy to the reading. This is also optional of course, and there are other ways for your querent to add their energy to the reading, without actually touching the cards, For example, they could tell you when to stop shuffling, or indicate the cards they want to choose from the pile.

Whilst to an outsider the cards may simply be pieces of cardboard, you will soon begin to feel a connection to them and see them as something more than mere objects. They do pick up and carry psychic energies. This is nothing to be afraid of and simply the way the cards work, but cleansing them every once in a while, or after doing lots of readings, is useful and some even consider it necessary.

There are many ways to cleanse your cards, and most make use of natural energies to do so. You can leave them out overnight in the light of the full moon, or the bright light of the sun. Be aware if you're doing the latter that some cards can bend a little in heat or humidity, so don't leave them for too long. Some people use crystals such as clear quartz or amethyst laid on top of the deck. If you do this, cleanse the crystal afterwards by passing it through running water. Smudging, or passing through the smoke from incense or even a fire, is a popular way to cleanse tarot cards, and is very effective. Many people use sage, although this is a Native American tradition and has been so widely appropriated that white sage is now an endangered species. Try to use a herb from your own cultural tradition, or look up the magical correspondences of the herbs you have in your kitchen. Rosemary or lavender are good, as are sandalwood or frankincense. Its fine to try a few different methods of cleansing your cards, and see what works best for you, and for your deck.

## *HOW TO READ THE TAROT CARDS*

Studying and reading the tarot can be a life's work, but all you really need to get started is a deck of cards, your intuition (a kind of inner knowing everybody has which goes beyond the intellectual) and some basic card meanings, which this book will give you. To do a tarot reading, we shuffle the cards and lay them out in a particular order, known as a spread. Each position in a spread has a meaning. A popular and simple three card spread, for example, includes cards representing the past, present and future. We then interpret the cards according to their position, using meanings developed over centuries as well as our own intuition. Becoming a good tarot reader means learning to synthesise these three elements – the meaning of the individual card, its position in the spread and in relation to the other cards in the spread, and the intuitive meanings which may seem to come out of the blue as you gaze at the cards.

Anyone can read the tarot cards, you don't have to have psychic skills or lots of book learning. All you need is the ability to still and open your mind and respond to the images you see before you. This book will guide you through the basics of tarot card meanings and how to combine them in a reading. Whilst learning the meanings off by heart using a book such as this one is useful, ultimately the best way to learn to use tarot cards is simply that, to use them. Do readings for yourself, for your friends and family.

The first thing to do before doing a reading, or using your cards at all, is to shuffle them. This comes naturally to some people, but others find it challenging. If you are not confident of your shuffling skills, there are other methods of making sure the cards are properly mixed up. For example, you could simply lay them face down on the table in front of you, and push them gently with a circling motion, so that they spread out into a "pool". Once you have moved them sufficiently, you can gather them back up into a stack, or simply choose the cards from the pool.

Some readers turn some of the cards upside down when shuffling so that in a reading they are "reversed". This can change the way they are interpreted, as reversals are seen as the shadow side of the energy of the card. Reversed cards may ask you to pay extra attention to that message, or show where energy is blocked and not quite ready to come into conscious awareness. This can be helpful, but some people find it confusing and see the full range of meanings in the card when it is upright. Reversed cards are often seen as the "negative" version of the card meaning, and so some people see them as alarming. However, the reversed meaning of a challenging card, such as the Tower or some of the Swords cards, can actually lighten the energy and make it less challenging. Once again, its a personal choice to include reversals in your readings, and there is no right or wrong answer. However its best to be consistent, so decide whether or not you want to work with reversals and then stick to it.

# GETTING TO KNOW YOUR TAROT DECK – SOME SIMPLE EXERCISES

Whilst you will want to start doing readings as soon as you can, it's a good idea to spend some time getting to know your cards and trying out different ways of using them. This allows you to build up a personal connection to the cards, and gain a knowledge of the tarot that goes deeper than simple book learning.

An excellent way to begin learning is to pull a single card when you get up each morning and keep the image in mind as you go through your day. At the end of the day, look in the book to review the standard meaning of the card, and see if how it relates to your day. You will find that patterns emerge – lots of Swords cards when you are studying for an exam, or lots of Major Arcana cards when you are going through a big change in life.

Another good technique is close observation. Choose a card, at random or one that you'd like to know better, and simply spend several minutes looking at it closely. Note as many details as you can – colours, clothing, posture, facial expressions. Look at the layout of the picture, where everything is in relation to everything else. Look at the background, there are often details there that are easy to miss. When you have observed the picture for a while, you can take a metaphorical step back and consider the mood, the attitude of any people in the image, and what meaning these imply.

If you read lots of books on the tarot or talk to lots of tarot readers, you may find that there are sometimes apparently contradictory meanings for the same card. This is because there are so many layers of interpretation to each card, and a meaning that resonates for one reader may leave another cold. When you are starting out, there are several places you'll want to look to get a sense of the possible interpretations for a particular card. The "LWB" or Little White Book, which comes with the deck, usually gives brief meanings for that specific deck, and some tarot cards come with a full book covering the particular meanings used by the creators of that deck. Other books, such as this one, give an overview of the traditional meanings for a card, and you can use these with any deck. As you gain experience with the cards, you will also find that you intuitively "sense" meanings for specific cards, during readings or meditations, and these can come across quite strongly. Personal intuitive meanings are by their nature subjective, but some see them as more meaningful than traditional interpretations for exactly this reason. They may work in a specific situation, for example when reading for a querent who has a specific reaction to a particular card.

All of these layers of meaning can be confusing, and you may find yourself wondering which is the "right" meaning. The answer is all of them, or maybe none. Every interpretation is equally valid, and the ones which resonate with you will be the ones which are right for you. The only answer is to practice reading, for yourself and others, and you will begin to get a sense of which method of interpretation works best for you. Some people prefer to memorise traditional meanings and use them as a jumping off point, others rely purely on the images and symbolism on the cards, and what their intuition is telling them that day. As you gain experience with the cards, you will naturally find yourself working in a particular way and responding to the meanings which ring true for you and your querent. Even the most experienced tarot readers are constantly discovering something new in the cards. The meanings are not fixed, and that is another of the great gifts of tarot. You may even find that the way you interpret particular cards changes and evolves over time, and that's fine too.

# CHAPTER TWO: THE MAJOR ARCANA

## THE JOURNEY OF THE MAJOR ARCANA

The twenty-two cards of the Major Arcana tell a story, describing the journey of the Fool as he moves from innocence to experience, from youth to maturity, from ignorance to enlightenment. This is a psychological and spiritual journey, giving us not only a deeper awareness and understanding of our worldly concerns but also a connection to universal energies.

This is not a journey which takes place on a uniquely linear plane - life goes in spirals, and we travel around the path many times in our lifetime. The spiritual wholeness of the final card, The World, leads straight back to the innocence of The Fool, which is generally seen as the beginning of the sequence, but also fits in at the end. The journey of the tarot works on both a macro and a micro level - it is the journey of a whole lifetime, from birth through youth, middle and old age to death, and also the multitudinous smaller journeys, spirals within an individual life.

The first Septenary, from the Magician to the Chariot, describes the journey to maturity. The Fool encounters the masculine and feminine energies of the archetypal Mother (the Empress) and Father (the Emperor) as well as the Magician and the High Priestess, who represent the spiritual aspects of the masculine and feminine. The Fool becomes aware that he is part of a cultural or religious tradition, meeting the Hierophant, who can help him to decide where s/he belongs. As he grows to maturity, he becomes aware of others and may fall in love, learning to relate to others and make choices for himself. Finally, the Chariot represents worldly ambition, as the Fool gains the power to achieve his goals.

However, achieving our goals doesn't always feel as satisfying as we might have hoped. Sometimes we get all that we ever wanted and wonder why we are not happy. Sometimes we don't get anything we wanted and simply wonder why. We begin to question our assumptions and social conditioning, why we think the way we do, whether there is more to life than we've been led to believe. This is the journey of the Second Septenary, as the Fool begins to question his path in life and to seek a deeper level of meaning. He discovers their inner Strength and develops a sense of right and wrong (Justice). He begins to look inwards, as the Hermit, and to seek his own wisdom and path in life, as he gains in maturity and experience. He begins to understand that life's ups and downs are not always of our making, encountering the Wheel of Fortune, and at the same time meeting the paradox that we may have more control over life than we assume. He may retreat for a while, shift his perspective and even find his world turned upside down, becoming the Hanged Man. This change in worldview may lead to a time of endings, of letting go of past ways of acting and being, as in the Death card. We have to let go of the old, to make way for the more meaningful life that we seek. This new freedom is reflected in the following card, Temperance, which represents the renewed balance between consciousness and unconscious, and is one of the calmest and most harmonious cards in the major Arcana.

In the final Septenary the Fool looks beyond his individual growth, and begins to wrestle with universal energies, coming to a deeper level of awareness and therefore a more profound ability to create change. Encountering the Devil, he becomes aware of the ways that we give away our power, to other people or to our own expectations, and the Fool is challenged to take back that power. The Tower follows, a breaking down of inner and outer structures which may feel painful (especially if we resist it), but which clears the way for a greater understanding. The Star brings a time of calm - coming through the disruption of the Tower brings a sense of relief and a renewed sense of trust and faith in the universe. The worst may have happened, but we have not only survived but thrived. The Fool meets the dreamy energies of the Moon and may get sucked into that shadowy and uncertain realm, but the clarity of the Sun helps him to connect to his inner truth, and find ways to express it. The Judgement card symbolises this rebirth and ability to follow our highest calling, leading finally to the fulfilment and integration of the World. Of course, nothing in life is static, and the completion of the World card opens the way for the next chapter, bringing us back to the Fool at the beginning of his journey.

We may not encounter the cards in this linear sequence when we do readings (although sometimes we do, and  is always a sign that your path is unfolding as it should). However knowing the story and the journey we take means that when Major Arcana comes up in readings, we have a sense of where we are on our journey, and what the next lessons might be. We can keep the journey in mind as we consider each of the Major Arcana cards individually.

# INDIVIDUAL CARD MEANINGS FOR

# THE MAJOR ARCANA CARDS

## 0 THE FOOL

Keywords: Free spirit, a leap into the unknown, a new beginning, the unexpected

The Fool card shows a young person, standing on the edge of a cliff. He carries little baggage and ignores the dog, symbolising conscious awareness, who barks at his feet. The Fool is spontaneous and lives fully in the moment. His actions may seem like folly to others, but he has faith and trusts that all will comes right in the end. He is open to whatever gifts come his way and has no expectations, either good or bad. Indeed he is acting from his impulses, which may or may not prove to be right. The Fool moves towards change without knowing what kind of change it is or where he will end up, and this doesn't worry him. In fact, he welcomes the unknown, the excitement of a new journey with no particular destination in mine. The Fool is playful and open, not minding that this can also make him vulnerable or even foolhardy. The archetype of the Fool appears in many mythologies, as a trickster, reminding kings and heroes of their truth and not letting them get caught up in their own hubris. Sometimes, the apparently foolish are the only ones able to speak truth to the established powers. We also see the importance of the Fool when we note that he is the only one of the Trumps to have survived the transition to the modern deck of playing cards. Just like the Joker, the tarot Fool travels where he will through the pack of cards and doesn't follow any rules.

Reversed or shadow aspects of the Fool include a tendency to rush ahead without any awareness of the possible consequences. On the other hand, it may mean remaining in your comfort zone and refusing to try anything new or simply taking life too seriously, being cynical or pessimistic.

When the Fool comes up in a reading, a new adventure is about to begin. It's time to take a risk, to leap off the cliff often depicted in this card and trust that the path will be there to catch you. This is the card of following your bliss, of ignoring the expectations of others and doing what feels right for you. Listen to the cosmic messages of the universe and also to your own inner voice, then take a deep breath, and jump!

# 1 THE MAGICIAN

Keywords: Inner power, creativity, focus, attention, putting ideas into action

The Magician is a powerful figure, with the forces of the universe at his command, shown by the position of his arms. His right arm is held high to receive the energies of spirit, and his left hand points downwards, indicating that he brings those energies into everyday reality, and makes something tangible with them. His magic wand symbolises authority and confidence, the masculine or active energies we use to do our work in the world. On his table are the tools of the four suits of the Minor Arcana, showing his inner resources and talents. The Magician is single-minded and pure in his intentions and represents our ability to establish our priorities, focus on our goals and then take action to make them a reality. The Magician is both potential and experience and reminds us that when we act from a higher purpose, we connect to our highest self. He represents knowledge, learning and initiative, all bringing the potential for growth. Like the Fool, the Magician can be a trickster, and in early tarot decks, he was often shown as a conjurer or even a juggler. He is the archetype of the wizard, the wise magician who can change the world with his powers. In some decks, he is depicted as a shaman, who walks in the otherworld and brings its wisdom back to the mundane world.

Reversed or shadow aspects of the Magician can be trickery or deceit, acting from self-interest or for personal gain, and not respecting the needs of others. Using his power to dominate others or for selfish reasons results in the Magician losing his connection to the higher power which guides him. The shadow side of the trickster is the conman who cheats others for his own personal gain.

In a reading, the Magician tells you that you have what you need to make your dreams a reality. It's time to take action to realise your potential, to tap into your willpower and inner vitality. Have confidence in yourself and your abilities, and use the power of your conscious mind to achieve your goal. Concentrating on the project at hand, whilst also listening to the wisdom of your higher self, is the best way forwards.

## *2 THE HIGH PRIESTESS*

Keywords: intuition, secret knowledge, deeper meaning, hidden self

The High Priestess is a mysterious figure, connected with dreams, intuition and the messages of the unconscious. She is the Magician's opposite, the power of the unconscious mind, the shadowy inner self and the power of receptivity and stillness. As the keeper of ancient and eternal wisdom, she represents knowledge and awareness of the mystery of life, as well as collective and personal memory. The black and white pillars often shown on either side of her throne symbolise light and dark, inner and outer, thought and feeling, all the dualities which we

44

experience in our lives. Behind the curtain, she guards the mystery which brings them into balance. Her connection to the moon, shown in her headdress and also in the crescent moon at her feet, reminds us that life moves in cycles, the ebb and flow and that the quiet dark is just as important as the times of light and action. She is the archetype of deep feminine understanding, connected to wisdom goddesses such as Sophia and Isis, and she understands the deep power of the unconscious and of the underworld. A historical or legendary source for this card is the story of the woman who was once elected Pope (strictly against the rules of the Catholic Church), only being revealed as a woman when she gave birth during an Easter celebration, and until the eighteenth century, this card was called the Papess. The persistence of this story reflects the importance of the feminine archetype even in the male-dominated medieval Christian church and also reflects the meaning of the High Priestess as a mysterious figure whose full self must remain hidden.

Reversed or shadow aspects of the High Priestess can be an inability to connect to our dreams or listen to our intuition, thinking literally or superficially, and assuming that we already know everything. The reversed High Priestess might also indicate that we have been passive for too long, and need to take action to change our situation.

When she comes up in a reading, the High Priestess says that now is not the time for action. This is a time to go inwards, to listen to your intuition which is likely to be strong right now. There may be hidden potential or a new possibility about to come to light. This is a time when you can connect to the inner mysteries, to a sense of something greater than yourself.

# 3 THE EMPRESS

Keywords: fertility, creativity, generating new life, abundance, fruition, feminine energy

The Empress is the energy of the archetypal Mother, bringing new life to birth and embodying the fertility and abundance of nature. She is often shown as a pregnant or surrounded by the fruits of the harvest, showing the luxuriant energy of life and all its bounty. She speaks of creative abundance, of the fulfilment of our heart's desires, of the pleasures of the senses. Her sceptre of power is topped by a globe, reminding us that we create, literally bring into being, our own world. The Empress symbolises the passionate, even sensual approach to life, the power to give and take experience and emotions without limit or restriction. The stream often depicted at her feet symbolises both the unconscious, connecting her back to the High Priestess, and the waters of life, which ensure that everything grows and flourishes. She shows us how we can use our imagination and creativity to generate ideas and to birth them in reality. She also reminds us of the need to balance patience and action, to allow the harvest to develop in its own time so that it can grow to its full potential. The Empress represents synthesis and harmony, the unity which is born from the dualities of light and dark, action and receptivity. She is firmly rooted in our present experience and our connection to the world around us but also holds an awareness of our potential and what we are able to create.

Reversed or shadow aspects of the Empress may be struggling to connect with our emotions or ability to nurture ourselves and others, not giving others the space they need to be themselves, and sometimes destroying instead of creating. Reversed, the Empress might also suggest an over-abundance rather than a lack of emotions.

In a reading, she indicates a time of abundance, creativity and growth. You may be bringing a new project into being, nourishing and nurturing it into reality. It's a time to connect to nature and to the powers of your senses. She reminds us that abundance is not just about the material, but about gratitude for the many gifts life gives us each day. Take time to nourish whatever is most important to you, focusing your energy and attention on it.

## 4 THE EMPEROR

Keywords: authority, power, control, boundaries, masculine energy

The Emperor is the archetypal energy of the father, an authority figure who seeks to control and organise. He may represent social conformity, rules and regulations and the need to maintain order. He is confident in his right to rule and expects others to follow his lead. He is the master builder and the force of civilisation, bringing order to chaos and setting the rules which ensure that society functions successfully. He sets standards and social expectations and expects them to be met. The Emperor is a man of reason and logic, as well as action. He protects all those within his care, bringing security and comfort to his people. He has served his time on the battlefield and still wears his armour under his robes, ready to defend his people if he needs to. Now he represents the establishment and the social order, the father as guide, protector and provider. He is often seen as a very traditional, perhaps even old-fashioned, version of the father archetype as somebody rather remote and distant, who makes the rules and enforces discipline. A more positive approach is to see the Emperor as the creator of boundaries, helping us to know who we are as an individual and what our place is in the world. Most of us need to interact with mainstream society, to a greater or lesser extent, in order to live our daily lives, and we need to conform to certain behaviours to be accepted into that society, such as not harming others.

Reversed or shadow aspects of the Emperor include a tendency to control others, getting angry or defensive if our authority is challenged, becoming aggressive or dominating. On the other hand, the Emperor reversed can mean an inability to make decisions or take control of the situation.

In a reading, the Emperor asks you to look at your boundaries, and to your sense of inner authority. Are you in control of your life or are you trying to control those around you? It might be time to take on a leadership role, or to get clear about your direction and purpose in life. The Emperor indicates a need to take responsibility for yourself, to become the ruler of your own life. Getting organised and focused are also indicated by this card.

## *5 THE HIEROPHANT*

Keywords: tradition, spiritual knowledge, teaching, education, group awareness

The Hierophant is a priest-like figure, usually shown with one or two acolytes or students who receive the knowledge and traditions he passes down. He symbolises established knowledge, the cultural and religious beliefs which inform our view of the world. His beliefs and ideas have been proven over time, which gives them authority and power but may also make them feel restrictive or rigid. The original name for this card was the Pope, linking it to the inner wisdom of the Papess or High Priestess, and this card can be seen as the outer manifestations of that wisdom, the church or belief systems which guide our society. However many people are now rejecting the established churches and choosing to follow their own spiritual path and ideally, the Hierophant is an inner teacher, the part of ourselves which seeks to understand the mysteries of the universe and the powers that guide us. He guides us through rituals and celebrations, the events which mark the rhythms of our lives and give them meaning. The Hierophant also represents groups and structures in society, the desire to conform and feel part of a group. This sense of belonging can bring security or restriction, and again as our inner guide, the Hierophant asks us to question our beliefs, not to mindlessly follow the ideas of others. We can draw on the wisdom of our traditions whilst also adapting it to work better in our own lives. Sometimes this card can refer to a giving away of responsibility, sticking to the rules in order to avoid thinking for ourselves about what is right and wrong.

Reversed or shadow aspects of the Hierophant may be intolerance of the beliefs of others, or blindly accepting other people's ideas, group or personal dogma. The Hierophant reversed can also suggest rebelling for the sake of it, rejecting the traditional or conventional but not replacing it with anything meaningful, or developing our own original ideas.

When the Hierophant comes up in a reading, you may be feeling drawn to a spiritual or religious tradition, or feeling the need to rebel against it and seek your own wisdom. You may be considering your group identity and wondering where you belong, or considering your beliefs and worldview, and how they inform your choices in life.

## 6 THE LOVERS

Keywords: relationship, love, inner and outer union, bringing together of opposites, choice

In the Lovers, we meet the "other" for the first time and must learn how to relate to others. The Lovers represent union, both with another person and within ourselves, and the coming together of opposites. This card is about forming bonds and connections, in romantic relationships and also more generally. Relationships with others, whether close and lasting or fleeting, offer us opportunities for growth, for getting to know ourselves better and also for learning to focus on something beyond ourselves. Whilst it's tempting always to interpret this card in that context, it's important to remember that we also have a relationship with ourselves, and this card also symbolises integrating the masculine and feminine (we all have both, although we do not always express them equally) within ourselves. The angel shown in many of the more modern versions of the Lovers represents a mediating force, helping us to balance our inner and outer dualities. When we feel complete and accepting of ourselves, we can meet others as a more honest version of ourselves, avoiding the projections which can influence our relationships. Our active or masculine side is often directed by our feminine or unconscious side, and this card symbolises this dynamic and the way it guides our actions.

The shadow or reversed aspects of the Lovers might be difficulty trusting or opening up to others, refusing to accept conflicting aspects of ourselves, and also expecting another person to complete or heal us rather than taking responsibility for our own emotional wellbeing. It may suggest being in a relationship for the "wrong" reasons, such as a fear of being alone, or love as a destructive rather than a unifying force.

In a reading, this card can be easy to interpret – it indicates a relationship, the strengthening of a bond with a loved one, perhaps a commitment or even marriage. However, it can also indicate the need to make a choice, often between staying in your comfort zone or moving towards a new level of maturity. Sometimes it represents the need to bring the masculine and feminine, the active and receptive, sides of ourselves into balance.

# 7 THE CHARIOT

Keywords: action, momentum, power, focus, determination, achievement, purpose

The Chariot is the card of victory, of being in control and achieving your goals. It can mean bringing the opposing energies sometimes indicated by the Lovers under control, by force or otherwise, and using this energy to move forward in pursuit of your ambitions. The two animals pulling the vehicle depicted in the card are often different colours or trying to go in different directions. As the driver of the Chariot, you need to keep them in balance, for both are necessary to move forward. Driving such a vehicle at speed requires total control over the animals, and so this card symbolises strong willpower. The charioteer is the victorious hero, who conquers all that he sets out to conquer. This card indicates worldly success achieved through sustained effort. Its a card of determination and enthusiasm, and often indicates the potential for leadership and accomplishment. There is always movement with the Chariot, a constant moving forwards in a dynamic balance. The sphinxes or horses once again represent the dualities within us, thinking and feeling, and acting and reacting. The Chariot can symbolise our "persona", the mask we create as we grow up which allows us to deal with the outside world and hide the parts of ourselves we are not so comfortable with.

The reverse or shadow side of the Chariot may be controlling yourself or others too much, or not enough, and having little sense of purpose or direction. It may also mean trying too hard to achieve a goal which is not right for you at this time. You may need to change your perspective or path, rather than following a course simply because it's the one you are already on.

When the Chariot comes up in a reading, you are likely to be in pursuit of a goal, probably with single-minded focus and a sense of purpose. Success is secure as long as you keep the momentum going, and keep your inner and outer selves, your thoughts and emotions, in balance. This is the card of the ego, which organises and controls our persona and allows us to act in the world but can become rigid and fearful if we are not careful.

## 8 STRENGTH

Keywords: inner strength, compassion, gentle control, patience

Like the Chariot, the Strength card symbolises willpower and our ability to control the circumstances around us and use them to our advantage. However the strength represented here is not forceful control or power over others, but rather power from within, a kind of gentle control which is patient and tolerant of the needs and desires of others. This card usually shows a woman who has tamed a lion or other wild beast, which allow her to touch it. The animal symbolises our inner "wild side", our animal instincts. Our strength and power come from those instincts and this card symbolises the power to use them wisely, rather than allowing them to take over, so that we act without conscious consideration. In some ways this card can be seen as balancing our conscious minds with our unconscious instincts, to make the best use of both of them. This is a strength of "allowing" rather than forcing, of using our inner rather than our physical powers. We can follow and fulfil our desires without allowing them to take us over or to hurt others, by transforming the devouring energies of our inner wildness into something in harmony with our higher self. The strength shown here is the strength to face life, especially when we are faced with challenges or change, with hope, able to see the opportunities or growth rather than becoming overwhelmed or giving up.

The reverse or shadow aspects of this card can be a lack of self-control, courage or integrity, being forceful or aggressive, and also losing focus and scattering your energy. It can also mean a lack of self-belief or loss of confidence in yourself.

In a reading, this card shows that you have this strength, and do not need to force others to bend to your will. Instead, you can inspire others with your tolerance and compassion. You can be guided by your instincts without being overtaken by them. This is a time to balance action and the urge to move forwards with intuition and the need for patience. You may be becoming aware of the power of your emotions and the need to use it consciously.

# 9 THE HERMIT

Keywords: solitude, inner wisdom, truth, patience, experience

The Hermit card shows a mature figure, carrying a lamp which symbolises inner wisdom, the knowledge we have built up with our life experience, which we can now use to light our way. The Hermit is a contemplative figure, who looks inwards and reflects on his knowledge in order to find the way forward. He is not in a rush and knows that true wisdom takes time. In fact the Hermit also symbolises the past, and old age, the power of time to bring change and growth. After the worldly cards of the first stages of the Fool's journey, now the Hermit asks us to draw on our inner strength and look within, to explore our own unconscious minds, to figure out what is most meaningful to us and use that awareness to guide our choices. He holds his lamp in his right hand, symbolising this conscious awareness of our inner wisdom. The Hermit symbolises humility before a higher power, and he knows that the more he learns, the more he realises he doesn't know. The Hermit is another powerful and deep-rooted archetype, and throughout history, people have withdrawn from society in order to contemplate the greater mysteries, like the medieval hermit living in a cave or the woods. On a symbolic level, the Hermit represents the idea that by withdrawing from the demands and concerns of the outer world, we can connect more deeply to our inner world. The Hermit asks us to consider where we are focusing our attention and energy, and whether it is truly worth our time.

The shadow or reversed aspects of the Hermit can be a feeling of isolation or loneliness, feeling uncomfortable with your inner self and unwilling to look within. You may find yourself taking refuge in meaningless activities or spending time with others to avoid the unsettling call of your higher wisdom.

When the Hermit appears in a reading, he indicates a time of quiet, calm introspection, even solitude. You are likely to be seeking something, perhaps a greater understanding of your life so far or your future path, or simply a deeper awareness of your place in the universe. It may be time to reevaluate your priorities, values and goals, especially if they are not allowing you to grow.

## 10 THE WHEEL OF FORTUNE

Keywords: cycles, change, ebb and flow, ups and downs

The Wheel of Fortune is a traditional image showing the ups and downs of life – sometimes the circumstances around us are positive and things seem to go our way, and at others times we may struggle or feel that we are unable to make progress. Often we do not have any control over these changes, and so the meaning of this card is also acceptance, as well as fate or destiny. This card can symbolise the natural rhythm of life, the season of growth and the season of fallow energy, and the awareness that both are necessary to keep us in balance. The Wheel teaches us when to go with the flow, when to endure, and how to understand out situation deeply enough that we know which of these approaches will serve us best. We are part of something bigger than ourselves, and an awareness of the Wheel of Fortune can give us a glimpse of this greater pattern. In history and mythology, the Wheel of Fortune can symbolise both the natural and mysterious laws of the universe, the seemingly random events of life, and also our attempts to influence those laws and change our apparent fate. As the halfway point of the Major Arcana sequence, the Wheel shows us how our lives are balanced between elements that we can control and a kind of fate or destiny which is more mysterious.

The reversed or shadow aspects of the Wheel of Fortune can be procrastination and passivity, assuming that our fate is out of our hands and there is nothing we can do to change it. Fighting or resisting necessary change can also be a negative manifestation of this card.

In a reading, the Wheel can indicate a time of change, a period when things seem to be happening beyond your control and you have no choice but to go with them. On the other hand, it can indicate a time when you feel stuck and don't seem to be able to move forward. Either way, the message of this card is often that whilst we may not be able to choose the circumstances around us, we can choose how we react to them and use the energy available to us.

# 11 JUSTICE

Keywords: balance, integrity, harmony, right action, equilibrium

As you might expect, Justice is the card of right and wrong, or right action and the repercussions of our actions. It can symbolise the structures around this in our society, such as the law, but on a deeper level, it speaks of our ethics and morality, the need to act with integrity and honesty. It symbolises impartiality, fairness, balance and objectivity, the need to act from our head, not from our heart. The principles of social or legal justice are more correctly ruled by the Emperor, whereas the Justice card represents a kind of cosmic equilibrium, the forces which keep the universe in balance as well as our individual lives. This can be a card of karma, of accepting that all of our choices and actions have consequences and that even if they are unintended, they are still our responsibility. This can be a liberating process, as it frees us from constantly repeating the same life patterns until we have learned the lessons of that past behaviour, and Justice brings us an awareness that our apparent free will is shaped by our past actions. Justice doesn't simply ask that we balance all the dualities and contradictions within us, but accept that each has something to teach us. We need to listen to and accept all viewpoints, to acknowledge them all as equally valid. The objectivity of Justice helps us to understand the ups and downs of the Wheel of Fortune and to bring those extremes into harmony.

The reversed or shadow aspects of Justice can be refusing to take responsibility for our actions or to accept the consequences of our decisions, and also leaping ahead to make a decision without considering all the facts. Acting from our heart rather than using our head is also relevant here.

In a reading, the appearance of the Justice card may indicate the need to make a decision, or perhaps to consider the causes and effects of your actions. It indicates a need to take responsibility and to act with integrity, doing what we know to be right rather than what is easy. When we see the Justice card, we need to consider how to honour our contradictions and bring ourselves into harmony.

## 12 THE HANGED MAN

Keywords: release, surrender, shift in perspective, sacrifice, suspension

The Hanged Man is a mysterious figure, unsettling to some as he appears to be in an uncomfortable position. However, in most of the images of this card, he looks peaceful and even happy. The Hanged Man is a paradox, for he teaches us that sometimes, the best way to succeed is to stop trying. After the turning inward of the last few cards and the uncomfortable truths we may be discovering about ourselves, the Hanged Man brings a period of peace. We need to suspend our actions for a while, reverse our perspective and surrender to what comes. This is a card of knowing when the time is right, and not doing anything until that time. The power of the Hanged Man lies in his stillness, his openness to a new way of being, and his ability simply to wait for the right time. He teaches us to re-frame our experience, to seek the positive in a challenging situation or the reality of an illusion. He can also show us our place in the bigger picture, allowing us to see beyond our individual concerns and connect to something greater than ourselves. This new perspective can allow us to sacrifice some of those individual concerns, especially those which are proving to be meaningless and make space for a clearer sense of who we really are. The Hanged Man can bring a kind of independence of thinking, an ability to release our social conditioning and follow the path of our hearts.

Reversed or shadow aspects of this card include holding on to a way of being which no longer serves us or refusing to consider change. We may not be willing to make the necessary sacrifices which will allow us to move forward, or we may sacrifice too much of ourselves or take on a victim mentality.

When he comes up in a reading, the Hanged Man tends to indicate a time when trying or taking conscious action to change our situation will not help. We need to release, to let go of our urge to control and allow events to unfold as they will. This is a card of patience and stillness, of allowing ourselves simply to be.

## 13 DEATH

Keywords: release, endings, transformation, change

Many fear this card, and perhaps with good reason, for it carries a powerful energy. It rarely indicates a literal death, but it does mean a change, a process of release and transformation which we must allow to happen if we are to move forward. Endings inevitably bring sadness, but almost every image of this card shows a new dawn beyond the skeleton, a new beginning on the horizon. In most cases, the changes heralded by the Death card are natural changes, for ultimately death is simply a part of life, one of life's few inevitablilities. The cycle of life, death and rebirth is the foundation of all things, and it must be acknowledged as such. The Hanged Man brings us to an awareness of what we need to release, and the Death card describes that process of release. It may be messy and painful, it may be a relief and a source of joy, but either way it is powerful and brings about deep transformation. We live in a world that often encourages us to ignore what is difficult, but it is there that the greatest power and potential lies. Death is usually seen as something to be feared, but it is actually the unknown that we fear, for who can really know what happens after we die? Symbolically, our ego resists change because of this same fear of the unknown. The image of dawn in the background of the card shows the positive potential of the unknown, the chance to experience life in all its glory.

The shadow or reversed aspects of the Death card can be resistance to change, stagnation and inertia, and holding on to worldly power or possessions to avoid the challenge of transformation and growth.

In a reading, the Death card indicates a process of inevitable change, and the need to acknowledge it rather than resisting or fighting against it. Whether it's an outdated emotional pattern or a job we no longer enjoy, saying goodbye to the past is the only way to move into our future. Sometimes we may be held back by unresolved feelings from our past, and acknowledging and releasing these clears the space for a new beginning.

# 14 TEMPERANCE

Keywords: balance, harmony, union of opposites, health

Temperance brings a calm energy after the powerful transformation of Death, a sense of inner union which comes from having faced our fears. Often shown as an angel pouring water between two containers, Temperance brings a sense of equilibrium and flow. She represents the principle of guiding and blending the dualities we have confronted in the last few cards, combining them to produce a sense of harmony. We are able to combine spontaneity with the knowledge we have gained so far and move beyond the restrictive masks of the ego self. The word "Temperance" comes from the Latin "temperare" which means "to mix" or "to combine properly". We do not just throw everything in together, we allow the process of combining to flow in its natural sequence. Like so many others in the second Septenary, this a card of allowing energies to flow rather than trying too hard or forcing them. Change comes when the time is right when all the pieces are in the right place and can come together in the most productive way. This card is often linked to rainbows, for example through the iris flowers shown in the image below and the resemblance of the angel to the Greek goddess Iris, goddess of the rainbow. The rainbow is a symbol of new life, of something magical seemingly created from nothing. It shows the energy of life which comes after the process of Death, our new awareness of our connection to the greater universe.

Reversed or shadow meanings of this card include being self-centred or going to extremes, mood swings or unstable actions, chaos or lack of self-control. Temperance reversed can indicate that you keep the various parts of your life too separate and risk becoming fragmented or losing a sense of who you are as a whole person.

When it appears in a reading, the Temperance card can mean a need for moderation or balance, for not going to extremes. It can indicate a time when we are in our "flow", able to connect to a deeper sense of self and act from that, bringing creative energy and a sense of being in touch with our true self. This card can also relate to health and a sense of wellbeing.

## 15 THE DEVIL

Keywords: power, bondage, freedom, materialism

The Devil is another card which many find challenging, with its often unsettling images of a horned figure presiding over two figures in chains. However look closer and you'll see that the chains are loose, and that the figures could remove them if they chose. Whilst this card can indicate feeling trapped or controlled, it also shows us that we have the ability to break our bonds. Often the Devil symbolises our shadow side, the parts of ourselves that we prefer to deny or ignore. We may be overly concerned with appearances or social status, with things that are not really meaningful and which take our power away from our spiritual growth. The Devil symbolises not only a focus on the material and meaningless, but also the illusion that nothing exists beyond that, a denial of the gifts and mysteries of spirit. The illusions of the material realm limit and restrict us, and can become addictions, in extreme cases. They do not bring true satisfaction, and so we keep going, thinking that the next shiny new thing will be the one that finally makes us happy. Once we acknowledge these feelings and the futility of this quest, we are released and can use the energy we reclaim for something genuinely meaningful. Like the Death card, facing our fears and challenges here is a powerful experience, one that can transform us deeply. The Devil card signifies the life force which we lock away in our shadow side or unconscious mind, and the ability to unlock it.

The shadow or reversed meaning of the Devil tends to mean giving in to our shadow side, focusing only on the shallow or superficial and ignoring the pull of anything deeper. On the other hand, it can mean the process of releasing our chains and taking back our power, acknowledging the shadow self.

In a reading, the Devil asks us to look to our power, and where we give it away. It may indicate that we are too caught up in the material and are neglecting our deeper self, or that we are ignoring our true self in an attempt to conform to the expectations of others. Either way, we are called to break our bonds and release our power.

# 16 THE TOWER

Keywords: breaking down, release, revelation, structures

Another unsettling card, the Tower shows figures being struck by lightning and falling from a high tower. It can indicate unexpected and even unwelcome change and upheaval or crisis over which we have no control. It often reflects the truism that bad luck seems to come in phases so that everything happens at once and we are left floundering as we try to deal with it all. On a deeper level though, it symbolises the need to break out of the structures we have built for ourselves, to change outdated patterns which no longer serve us. Having faced our shadow in the Devil, the structure of our ego may have taken a blow, as we are forced the confront the walls we have built around ourselves. As these walls shatter, we may feel that we are left stranded, our sense of security and safety gone. However, when we open our eyes and look around, we realise that we can see further than we have ever seen before and that new possibilities, things we might not have even imagined, are opening up before us. The Tower symbolises an awakening, a time when illusions are shattered and seemingly permanent structures are proved to be flimsy or false. Whilst this can be distressing, now you have the opportunity to build something stronger, and also more flexible, in accordance with your own values instead of the expectations or needs of others. This card can also symbolise a flash of insight or even enlightenment, a breaking open of awareness which gives us a much broader view of life.

The reversed or shadow meanings of the Tower include avoidance of change, refusal to understand or allow your awareness to grow, and holding on to rigid attitudes and entrenched ideas. It can also suggest a milder version of the upright meaning, a less dramatic version of necessary changes.

When the Tower comes up in a reading, it inevitably indicates a time of change. Whilst this can be unsettling or even painful, it also usually brings revelation. We are broken out of our comfort zone, and possibilities open up around us. It's time to let go of what no longer works and build something more fulfilling.

## 17 THE STAR

Keywords: hope, optimism, trust, faith

A time of calm follows a time of upheaval. The Star brings a sense of relief and a renewed sense of trust and faith in the universe. The pool often shown in this card represents our connection to something greater than ourselves, and we can tap into this when we are in need of reassurance or inspiration. The Star symbolises hope and optimism, a sense that we are on the right path. The light of the Star is the light of understanding, awareness, and truth, stimulating our imagination and our sense of connection to something greater than ourselves. The universe, spirit, the divine – however we think of it or define it, we are offered a continuous supply of wisdom, of energy for growth and understanding. The Star shines above us to guide our way, showing us a deeper sense of meaning and direction in our lives. The pool often shown in the Star card symbolises our connection to the unconscious mind, on both a personal and a collective level, and we can connect to the waters of the pool by tuning in to our still inner voice. The Star inspires us to bring the gifts of the unconscious into tangible reality, through our creative talents. Our inner transformation and newfound connection to the source of life (symbolised by the pool in the image) brings the potential to the way we work and act in the world. This is a card of inner calm and serenity, bringing healing and a holistic awareness. All the masks have fallen away (which is why the figure in this card is almost always nude), we know our place in the universe and our true self.

The shadow or reversed meanings of the Star include denying our talents and inner truths, losing ourselves in idealism without bringing our ideals into reality. It may mean insecurity, losing hope or taking a pessimistic attitude.

The appearance of the Star in a reading suggests an ability to connect to our deeper self and to trust that all will be well. Love and energy flow freely and are available to us as we need them, for ourselves or to share with others. This is a time to align ourselves with a higher consciousness, to grow in our connection to spirit, and to honour our creative imagination.

## 18 THE MOON

Keywords: cycles, imagination, shadow, illusion

The Moon can be a shadowy figure, indicating shadows and illusions as well as imagination and dreams. This card symbolises the unconscious mind and the darkness, which we often see as frightening. We fear the unknown, but it also brings great gifts of imagination and inspiration. The Moon symbolises the knowledge we hold deep in our cells, the embodied wisdom which goes beyond our intellect and connects us to our instincts and intuition. Intimately connected with our feeling self, the Moon asks us to listen to the wisdom of our emotions and to acknowledge their power. Delving deep into ourselves, we may encounter fears and delusions, perhaps old emotional patterns which no longer serve us and we can bring them into the Moon's gentle light and let them go. The Moon is connected with the cycles of growth and decay and asks us to pay attention to those cycles in our lives, learning when to let our energies build and when to release them. The darkness is just as important as the light, allowing us to nurture the seeds of new growth and also to rest and retreat when we need to. The Moon card always indicates the activity of the unconscious. This may be our personal unconscious minds, speaking to us through dreams, fears, and feelings, but may also be the collective unconscious. The Moon shows our connection to this more universal shadow, the aspects of it we connect to most deeply and how that connection affects us.

The shadow or reversed side of the Moon can be failing to acknowledge our feelings, imagination and sensitivity, ignoring the shadow, or paying too much attention to illusions and allowing them to rule us. Ignoring the pull of the unconscious means that it will simply try harder to get your attention, which can lead to distorted emotions and fears.

In a reading, the Moon suggests that this is a time when linear thinking will not work. Instead, you need to go with the flow, to follow your intuition and to let your inner voice guide you. It may be a time of psychic or intuitive awakening when you are learning to listen to new forms of knowledge. You may need to be careful not to be overwhelmed with fears or anxieties. Your instincts can guide you to know what is real and what is an illusion.

## 19 THE SUN

Keywords: creativity, enlightenment, confidence, optimism, joy

The light of the Sun can literally bring enlightenment, a sense of clarity and vitality which revitalises and energises us. This is a card of confidence and creativity, of letting yourself shine and of having your achievements recognised. It can be a card of understanding, enthusiasm and positive energy, and of getting to the heart of the matter. The Sun gives us vital and constant energy, a micro-regeneration each day which allows us to work in, and on, the warmth and light of our conscious growth. This is another card of good health (along with Temperance), of feeling invigorated, charged up and full of enthusiasm. There's a reason that so many cultures honour the Sun as a god or goddess, for it brings life to the earth, and on a symbolic level, consciousness to the self. Rather than a card of the controlling ego, the Sun symbolises our true, authentic self, without the masks or personas we sometimes rely on, hence the nudity of the child often shown in the card. The child is our inner child, the pureness of our being and the horse often ridden by the child symbolises power and vital force, the ability to move forward with confidence along our life's journey. In the Sun we are aware of the beauty of life, understanding the power of the life force in all its manifestations, experiencing life as pure energy. We feel joy, optimism and a sense of wonder, and radiate these feelings to those around us.

The reversed or shadow aspects of the Sun can be ignoring our inner child, a fear of trust or lack of confidence in ourselves. The Sun reversed suggest surviving rather than thriving, and a need for more illumination in our lives. The positive energy of the Sun is not lost but may become confused and less clear.

The Sun showing up in a reading is generally seen as a very positive omen, indicating a time when you are clear in your purpose, understanding and ability to shine. Masks have been set aside and you are able to let your true self shine through. You may find yourself the centre of attention, encouraging and inspiring others. It may also indicate a time of strong vital and physical energy.

## 20 JUDGEMENT

Keywords: inner calling, rebirth, awakening, forgiveness

Judgement is a card of awakening, of becoming aware of a higher purpose or calling which inspires you. There is an inner conviction, a sense of something you have to do, even – especially – if it is difficult or challenging in your current circumstances. The angel blowing the trumpet which features in many depictions of this card is the summons which calls us to a higher consciousness, a new level of awareness. This call is within us, a kind of yearning which bubbles up and demands attention, and also experience it as something outside us, coming from a force much greater and more mysterious than ourselves. The Judgement card symbolises rising up out of the restrictions of self-doubt and the expectations of others, bringing a kind of rebirth, the opening up of a new sense of self. Judgement can show you your true vocation or purpose in life, asking you to listen for what makes your soul sing and then find a way to follow that path. It can be challenging, but the potential rewards are great. This card can also indicate a more literal kind of judgement, perhaps a time of evaluating your life and making some necessary changes or releasing and guilt or sorrow we carry from the past so that we can move forward. Often we judge ourselves much more harshly than we judge others so this card is as much about forgiving ourselves as it is about forgiving others.

The reversed or shadow meanings of the Judgement card include being critical or judgemental of ourselves or others, and feeling disconnected from our spiritual awareness and stuck in the material, refusing to hear the call or trying to ignore it. It may also mean that you want to answer the call, but don't know what to do or where to begin.

In a reading, the Judgement card can indicate a time of rebirth, of answering the inner call, following the yearning of your heart to find fulfilment and a sense of purpose. Sometimes it indicates a literal judgement to be made, a truth to be found or a decision to be made. There is an energy of regeneration inherent in this card, which brings hope and the opening up of new possibilities.

## 21 THE WORLD

Keywords: completion, integration, accomplishment, fulfilment

The World is a card of completion, of everything coming together to achieve something that is greater than the sum of its parts. As the final card of the Major Arcana, it brings together the energies of all the previous cards, synthesising and integrating them. It symbolises wholeness, happiness and a deep sense of connection. This is not a static energy, but a dynamic balance. We are connected to the dance of life, free of the fears and doubts which may have held us back in the past and able to see both ourselves and the world around us more clearly. The World is the last numbered card of the Major Arcana, and as the end of the cycle, implies the beginning of the new one. This is why the Fool is sometimes referred to as card number twenty-two, as once we have reached the unity of the World, we step once more into our clearest, most spontaneous self, and begin again the spiral of growth. Like the universe, we are in constant movement, always part of the cycles of our inner self as well as the great cycles of the universe around us. The figure in the World card is the cosmic dancer, often seen as androgynous, having finally united all the dualities within. S/he moves with the cycles, endlessly flowing, transforming and renewing. The World and the Fool are the only two cards in the Major Arcana which show moving figures, connected to the great spiral of being which is part of us all, and of which we all form a part.

The shadow or reversed meanings of the World can be a refusal to acknowledge that a cycle has come to an end, stagnation and a refusal to move on, or keeping yourself isolated and cut off from the rest of the world.

When it appears in a reading, the World indicates the end of a cycle, the fulfilment of a goal, a dream realised. This is a time of satisfaction and contentment, of gratitude for what you have and the results of your efforts. When the World card comes up, it reminds us that we are part of something much bigger than our daily concerns and individual lives, and connects us to planetary and even cosmic consciousness.

# CHAPTER THREE: THE MINOR ARCANA

## THE STRUCTURE OF THE MINOR ARCANA

The Minor Arcana consists of four suits, each containing fourteen cards, numbered Ace through to Ten and then Page, Knight, Queen and King. Each suit connects to one of the four elements, fire, air, water and earth. According to traditional occult symbolism, each element represents a different area of life. Through the elemental energies, the cards of the Minor Arcana show the energies which play out in our everyday lives.

The suit of Wands connects to the element of fire. It symbolises action, passion, vision and creativity. Cards in the suit of Wands often relate to our work or other projects we put energy into.

The suit of Swords connects to the element of air. It describes the realm of the mind, our thoughts and ideas, and the way we communicate them with others. Traditionally the suit of Swords has symbolised conflict, and so some of the images can be unsettling, but conflict is only one of the meanings of the Swords cards.

The suit of Cups is linked to the element of water, the element of feelings, emotions and the imagination. The Cups cards show us the realm of dreams and the unconscious as well as the way we feel about and relate to others.

Finally, the suit of Pentacles brings it all into the realm of the material, the element of earth. The Pentacles cards deal with money, home and work, but also with our resources, values and sense of abundance.

# THE JOURNEY THROUGH THE

# NUMBER CARDS

Each of the numbers carries its own symbolism, and in combination with the element of the suit decides the meaning of the card. In general, the even numbers are harmonious whilst the odd numbers bring challenges. The basic numerological meanings are as follows:

- The Aces are the spark, the new beginning. They introduce the basic energy and message of the suit and are often seen as a divine gift.

- The Twos are a decision or a balance to be found, a need to integrate the dualities in our lives.

- Threes are the creation of something new, the opportunity to manifest the energy sparked by the Ace.

- Fours are the building of a solid structure and represent the natural order.

106

- Fives bring change and chaos and may bring tests and challenges.

- The Sixes bring balance and equilibrium, a sense of wholeness or completion.

- The Sevens bring a yearning for deeper connection, a process of initiation or transformation.

- The Eights connect us to rhythm and harmony, but also demand that we choose our priorities.

- Nines are the peak of their suit and can represent success and completion.

- The Tens are the end of the cycle, containing within them the seeds of the next cycle.

# THE COURT CARD FAMILIES

The Court card families, based on a rather medieval hierarchy of Page, Knight, Queen and King, are the "personality" cards of the tarot. The Page embodies the childlike, innocent experience of the elemental energy, and is often a messenger or student. They are learning about their element and are often absorbed in it. The Knight is on a quest to understand the energy of the element and to take it out into the world. They are seekers and explorers, always hoping for an adventure. The Queens hold the energy of their element, transforming it from within and inspiring others to do the same. The Kings are the masters of their element, wielding it in the world with authority and using their experience to help others. In a reading, Court cards can represent an actual person who is part of the querent's life, somebody influential who may affect the querent's experience or choices. They can also symbolise an aspect of the querent themselves, or a role they are playing or an energy they are embodying at the time of the reading.

# THE SUIT OF WANDS

## ACE OF WANDS

The Ace of Wands is the creative spark, an exciting new possibility opening up for you. The lightning rod of the Ace of Wands channels and focuses the energy of fire, making it available for the querent to follow their passion, create something new, or find a new and inspiring vision to carry them forwards. The divine gift of the Ace is a sense of optimism and purpose, and also a sense of meaning, of why we do what we do. We open up to new experiences and find meaning as well as pleasure in them, and perhaps a new sense of direction. This card can indicate listening to your intuition and becoming aware of a more spiritual side of life and to your self. It may mean the beginning of a process of spiritual development or a new level of creative experience.

## TWO OF WANDS

This can be a card of making a decision, of moving forwards towards a new goal. However it begins with preparation and evaluation, and so this card may indicate a need to consider your options, to look at all of your possible futures and choose your direction. The Two of Wands indicates that you are moving into your personal power, able to move forward with courage and originality and that the potential of the Ace is beginning to take form. This may mean moving out of your comfort zone, and the decision demanded by this card may be simply that, to move away from the familiar and onto a new path. When the Two of Wands comes up, it suggests that you are feeling restless, and there is a need to honour that restlessness, to prepare for movement even if you are not actually ready to move yet.

## *THREE OF WANDS*

The Three of Wands is a card of expanding your vision and exploring the unknown. It can indicate that you have achieved quite a lot already and that now is the time to evaluate those achievements and decide which of them to build on. You have stepped onto the path and maybe even travelled some way down it and now is the time to decide where it will lead you next. The Three is always a number of integration and the Three of Wands asks for the integration of what has gone before with what will come next. This means looking at the bigger picture and perhaps considering what is still unknown to you, calling on all of your knowledge and experience to see as clearly as you can. The Three of Wands is a card of foresight and also leadership, for in making your own choices you can inspire others to do the same.

## FOUR OF WANDS

The structure of the Four is seen as positive in the suit of Wands, as it contains the fire safely whilst also allowing it to burn consistently, for as long as it is fed. This card represents celebrations, home and a sense of security which brings contentment and excitement. These things fuel your inner fire, helping you to feel safe and confident enough to explore our creative self and to reach for your goals. This card can also indicate a time of rest, of gathering in the harvest of work done so far and enjoying the results before moving into the next phase. Four of Wands energy is productive and constructive, the energy of plans put into action and carried out successfully. Good results bring confidence and a sense of inner strength, a solid foundation which helps us to move forward.

## FIVE OF WANDS

The combination of the chaotic Five and the difficult to control energies of fire bring competition, minor annoyances which can cause stress or disruption, and a lack of focus. Your confidence and self-belief may be challenged and competition with others may cause confusion. There may be conflicting values or competing demands, leading to stalled progress and frustration. However, the chaos can also be helpful, allowing you to brainstorm creative strategies and solutions, finding a way to bring them together harmoniously and usefully. There may be tension or disorder, but these can be stimulants for growth and for a new way of thinking, as long as all parties involved are willing to be open and honest. The important thing is to accept that change is needed and work towards making the necessary changes. Denying the issue at hand will only compound it and lead to bigger problems.

## SIX OF WANDS

The Six restores harmony, and in the Six of Wands your achievements are finally recognised and the struggles of the previous card are resolved. It's a time when you can feel proud and enjoy the acclaim of others and the traditional meanings for this card include victory, conquest and success. It is a card of leadership, accomplishment and ambitions fulfilled, and also of the need to acknowledge the support of others in achieving your goals. Your victory is the result of your efforts and the efforts of those around you, a success that is earned and is all the sweeter for that. It symbolises the confidence that comes from using your abilities and talents not only for your own good but for the good of others, and the sense of satisfaction which follows. This brings a sense of ease and an ability to move forward into the future with confidence.

## SEVEN OF WANDS

The Seven of Wands symbolises courage in the face of opposition, the need to stand your ground and

have the courage of your convictions. Following the success of the Six, new challenges appear. In most versions of this card, the figure holds the higher ground, symbolising the solid and positive position brought by past efforts and successes. However, the figure is usually also beset from all sides and may be outnumbered. When this card comes up, you may need to look at where you are on the defensive and where you have the strength to stand and fight. There may be a change you are resisting and sometimes letting go of the resistance is all that's needed to remove the obstacles to your progress. You may be called on to act with the courage of your convictions, and also to evaluate your priorities.

## EIGHT OF WANDS

The Eight of Wands signifies movement or rapid change, events which bring growth but which may feel rushed or as if your feet don't have time to touch the ground. In most versions of this image, the eight Wands are flying high in the air, carrying you into an exciting new future. The key is to use this energy to achieve your goals, without speeding ahead and losing sight of your priorities or focus. To others, it may seem as if you are moving for the sake of it, perhaps without necessary planning or thought, but to you, it most likely feels like you are "on a roll", and need to make the most of the momentum that is being generated for you. As well as action and movement, this card may mean receiving news which changes your situation, and lots of changes happening at once.

## NINE OF WANDS

This is a card of sustained effort and willpower, of not just finding your own path but creating each step as you go along. The work may feel challenging but also has the potential to bring great reward, as you are able to break old habits of excessive fear or caution. The energy of the Nines is quite self-contained, and this card can also mean the courage and energy to create your own destiny, rather than following convention or the expectations of others. This is not always an easy road, and there may be times when you are on the defensive, feeling frustrated at having to fight your corner over and over again. The key is taking responsibility for resolving any past issues which still affect you, and making space for healing rather than retreating into your comfort zone.

## TEN OF WANDS

The Ten of Wands is a card of commitment and dedication, having the determination to achieve your goals. It can mean giving service to something greater than yourself, such as family or the wider community, and accepting that the hard work and responsibility are worth it. It may mean that you have chosen your direction, and are happy to do whatever it takes to get there. However, it can also symbolise feeling burdened,as if you've taken on too much and can no longer see the way forward clearly. It may be time to let some commitments go, or at least to re-evaluate your priorities. The most important tasks are those which allow you to be true to yourself and to your higher purpose. Anything which doesn't serve those may need to be released or delegated, especially if you are only taking responsibility for it out of habit.

## PAGE OF WANDS

When the Page of Wands appears he brings opportunities to feed your passion and creativity. He encourages you to try something new, just for the fun of it. He is playful, curious, and always makes the choice which seems like the most fun. The Page is restless and may be easily distracted, because he is exploring, learning, seeking his path, and doesn't want to miss out on anything. All of these traits are part of a process of learning who he is and what his purpose is in life, and he is still at the beginning of this journey. The Page of Wands may need to acknowledge that he may not yet have the knowledge or experience he needs to define his goal more clearly. The key is to enjoy the process of gaining this knowledge and make the most of all the opportunities that come his way.

## KNIGHT OF WANDS

The Knight of Wands is an adventurer, setting off on a quest purely for the joy of taking action. He may enjoy taking risks and tends not to think before he acts. This is not because of a lack of intelligence, more that he is so inspired and enthusiastic about the task at hand that he cannot wait to get started, and so optimistic that he cannot see what might go wrong. He may come across as insensitive or intolerant because he is so focused on his quest that he is not aware of the needs or desires of others. He may also come across as somewhat erratic, as his energies burn fiercely whilst he is inspired by a task, but quickly dissipate when he loses interest until the next exciting quest comes along. He is likely to be very good at starting things, getting all fired up and passionate, but then losing interest when the initial excitement dissipates.

## QUEEN OF WANDS

A confident and passionate woman, the Queen of Wands is someone who encourages and inspires others with her creativity and enthusiasm. She has learned to hold the fiery energies within and release them when the time is right so that enthusiasm is sustained and the goal can be reached. She is independent and sure of herself, full of confidence but not arrogance, with enough self-awareness to encourage others without feeling threatened by them. Like all of the fiery Courts, at times she may seem domineering or even forceful, and she is likely to have little patience with those who are unwilling to take a risk. She takes a positive and optimistic approach and may get frustrated with those who she sees as unnecessarily negative or too fearful, perhaps not realising that not everyone can be as strong-willed as she is.

## KING OF WANDS

The King of Wands is an assertive and charismatic leader, willing to take chances and inspire action in others. He clearly expresses his creative imagination and is good at bringing his vision into reality. Unlike the Queen, he is not keen on working behind the scenes or in pursuit of someone else's vision, preferring to inspire others to help him bring his own vision into reality. He is good at influencing others and may become domineering, refusing to compromise his vision. He has little patience with those who do not share his confidence and determination, and his clear sense of focus. He will always take charge and shape the situation in the way that he wants or which advances his own plans. Sometimes he may struggle to understand that there are quieter forms of strength which are just as powerful as he is.

# THE SUIT OF SWORDS

## ACE OF SWORDS

The Ace of Swords brings a burst of mental energy, new ideas and a sense of clarity. The divine gifts of this Ace include reason, logic, intellectual thinking and mental discipline. The single sword cuts through mental and psychic clutter and brings a clearer vision, an ability to perceive the truth and to understand it. It brings a well of mental energy which can be focused on developing ideas and communicating them, and the growth of conscious awareness. This is a card of rational analysis and objectivity, the need to step back from emotions and view a situation dispassionately. It can also symbolise a sense of space, mental or otherwise, which allows new ideas to reach up into our conscious minds, bringing also the ability to understand them and decide what to do with them. The Ace of Swords connects us with the source of our ideas and also of our ability to communicate them with others.

## TWO OF SWORDS

When the Two of Swords appears, it may mean that you are feeling stuck or in a stalemate, not knowing how to move forwards or perhaps unable to make a decision. This card symbolises our inability or reluctance to see the truth or to deal with it, and possibly a refusal to change our opinion, blindfolding ourselves as the image often shows. Being closed off from others in this way can leave us isolated and lonely, or can give us the mental space we need to resolve the issues we are facing. Sometimes the message of this card is simply to make a decision. There is no right and wrong here, simply different choices, and we need to choose one of them and move on. Uncrossing the swords means reawakening the heart, and this card can be about the need to balance your thoughts with your feelings, the pull of logic with your emotions.

## THREE OF SWORDS

The Three of Swords is one of those cards that many see as difficult, as most of the images of it show a heart pierced by three swords. It's true that this card can mean painful feelings or a struggle with difficult emotions, but it can also mean releasing old emotional patterns and using our mind and intellect to understand our feelings. Sometimes we allow ourselves to be dominated by feelings which have actually moved on, or by fears which are no longer relevant. Applying the creative thinking of the Three of Swords allows us to see more clearly, and to realise that our feelings are simply that, our feelings, a part of us but not the whole of us. When this card appears, its time to acknowledge our feelings, and then let them go. This card can also symbolise bringing thoughts and feelings into creative harmony.

## FOUR OF SWORDS

The regularity and structure of the Four mean bringing your thoughts into harmony, clearing your mind of clutter and finding some mental space. You may need some time to process your emotions after the shifts of the Three, to practise not taking things personally and finding some objectivity. Taking time out allows us to get a sense of perspective, perhaps to reassess our priorities and make sense of our situation. This is a card of rest, retreat, taking time for reflection and contemplation, of letting go of our striving for a while. Every now and then we all need a little introspection, a time to step back from the demands of daily life and check in with ourselves. We do not always need to be "doing" and being productive, sometimes it's important just to be, with no goal or effort in mind.

# FIVE OF SWORDS

The image of the Five of Swords usually shows a man walking away from a battlefield, perhaps carrying several swords and with the others lying on the ground. The airy clarity of the Swords is lacking and the energy is turbulent and confused. This card can symbolise defeat, a battle lost, or won through deception. It asks you to check your motivation and state of mind. Are you focusing on your own needs at the expense of others, or seeking a balance between the two? When the Five of Swords appears, it can indicate a time of communication breakdown or a lack of clarity. There can be a need to choose your battles, to reassess your priorities and put your energy only into that which is most important. Otherwise, you may find yourself with scattered energy and scattered thoughts, lacking the focus to move forward and carry out your plans.

## SIX OF SWORDS

Once again the harmonious Six restores harmony after the chaos of the Five, and the image for the Six of Swords usually shows one or more people in a boat being ferried across calm waters. This card symbolises transition or evolution, the truism that change may not be dramatic and exciting but may come gradually, as we work on our inner and outer growth. The six Swords are carried in the ferry boat, and they may symbolise the inner truths or burdens you carry forwards with you or the established ideas which help you to make sense of life. They may also be interpreted as treasured possessions, past pain being held on to, or valuable resources with which to pay the ferryman. Either way, they are in some way necessary to the voyage and the transition into the next stage of life.

## SEVEN OF SWORDS

The traditional meanings for this card include secrecy and cunning, possible deception or not being able to see the whole picture. It can indicate taking a subtle or even hidden approach rather than acting openly, perhaps keeping your plans to yourself. Sometimes there is an element of mistrust and when this card comes up, it's important to check in with your own motivations and those of the people around you. It may simply mean that the time is not yet right to share your ideas. Whatever level this card is working on, it implies a time of solitude and relying on your own inner resources, acting independently rather than relying on the support of others. The Sevens always symbolise a process, an energy which grows over time, rather than a single event, and the Seven of Swords suggests a process of getting clear about your ideas and how you are putting them into action.

## EIGHT OF SWORDS

In contrast to the movement of the Seven, the Eight of Swords usually shows a figure who is standing still, often trapped and surrounded by swords. This card suggests that you are feeling powerless, restricted, or simply confused. There may be a sense of insecurity or self-doubt, perhaps a reluctance to make a choice due to lack of confidence or overthinking all the options. All of these things can restrict your thinking, leading to indecisiveness and an inability to break out of these habitual patterns of thought. However, we may be less trapped than we think. In most of the images of this card, the figure is only loosely tied around the arms and there are gaps between the swords. Sometimes all you need to do is make the choice to break out, and you will find its easier than you expect so that the Eight of Swords is also a card of liberation.

## NINE OF SWORDS

The Nine of Swords shows us the challenges of this process of liberating your mind from the thoughts that hold you back. It indicates a time when you may be allowing your worries or anxieties to take over, imagining the worst and struggling to clear your mind. Like the previous card, it shows the power of the mind and the effect it can have on you, holding back growth due to imagined doubts and often unfounded fears. When the Nine of Swords comes up, there is a need to clear the mind, perhaps doing something physical which allows you to bypass the busy thinking brain. Rather than giving equal energy to worries or concerns which may not even happen, its time to sort through them and work out which are genuine and which are simply old habitual patterns of feeling and thinking.

## TEN OF SWORDS

The Ten of Swords shows the end of the cycle, often illustrated by a figure lying on the ground, with all ten swords in their back. One of the meanings for this card can be having a victim mentality, believing that everything is against you in a rather dramatic way. However, the regeneration of the Tens is also shown, with the lightening sky of a new dawn often shown beyond the figure. There is a need to accept and release the past, to let go of the patterns of thinking which keep you pinned down, clearing the way for a new beginning. The Ten of Swords can show a time of gathering and replenishing your energies, of recommitting to your path. It can also mean taking your ideas out into the world, teaching or sharing them with others, which is of course also a kind of release.

## PAGE OF SWORDS

The Page of Swords is setting out on his journey to gain knowledge of himself and the world around him, to understand the world and his place in it. He is determined, self-willed and perhaps somewhat detached, not quite ready to form close relationships with others yet. Instead, he is keen to make his own way, to be allowed to make his own mistakes if necessary. He is exploring his ideas, concepts and seeking his own truth, using his intellect and the powers of his mind in quite an abstract way, as he doesn't yet have the life experience to do otherwise. When the Page of Swords appears, you are likely to be practising using your mental energy and ability to communicate with others. This card can symbolise messages and new ideas which bring a new level of awareness, perhaps studying or learning something new which expands your horizons.

## KNIGHT OF SWORDS

This Knight is on a quest to fight for the truth and welcomes conflict as an opportunity to get closer to that truth. He is courageous and clever, always ready to defend his ideas and his honour, and always on the move. He has strong powers of logic and reason, often seeing the world as black and white and acting accordingly. Quick thinking and even impulsive, he has the courage of his convictions, to the point that he may struggle to let go of an idea even when it is proved wrong. He thinks quickly but not necessarily deeply, and may choose action based on a half-developed idea over a carefully planned strategy. His insistence on logic and objectivity may mean that he lacks tact and empathy with others, sometimes riding roughshod over individuals and their needs in order to achieve his goal.

## QUEEN OF SWORDS

Honest and astute, the Queen of Swords tells it like it is and doesn't flinch from the truth. Ideally, she transforms sorrow into wisdom by applying her powerful intellect to her emotional experiences, finding a sense of perspective and an ability to see the bigger picture. Her experience meeting the ups and downs of life has brought resilience and courage, as well as empathy for others and a heart connection which is not always present in the Swords cards. She is able to use logic and reason to quash any self-doubts or confused thinking and to help others to do the same. She is quick-witted and has a love of ideas, along with the maturity to develop them fully and share her understanding and wisdom with others. The Queen of Swords makes decisions quickly and with compassion, and lives by her ideals.

## KING OF SWORDS

Articulate and intellectual, the King of Swords sees straight to the truth of the matter and has excellent analytical skills. He is an intellectual leader and keen strategist, always acting from high ideals, high standards and a deep level of experience and understanding. At times this may mean that he seems to lack compassion or tolerance, and he may consider the greater good to be more important than the needs of the individual. He is a trusted adviser, forthright and reliable, who is able to be realistic as well as idealistic. He stands for law, order, discipline and sound judgement, and as such may come across as a strong authority figure who does not like to be opposed. When the King of Swords appears, its time to use your judgement and find some clarity about your situation, and then take decisive action.

# THE SUIT OF CUPS

## ACE OF CUPS

The Ace of Cups brings a rush of emotional energy or an opening up of the imagination. It can symbolise a return to the source of yourself, getting in touch with your unconscious mind through your dreams and intuition. There may be a new attraction or bond with another, an overflowing of feeling which feels exciting and full of promise. A new chapter is beginning in which relationships and connections with others, as well as connection to your own feelings and imagination, bring personal growth and a deeper connection to the spiritual side of life. This is a time to be open to new opportunities, to focus on and express your gratitude for what you have. You may be feeling a little vulnerable and sensitive, especially if there are strong emotional energies around you, so it's important to practise self-care and love yourself as well.

# TWO OF CUPS

When the Two of Cups appears, you may be making a soul connection with another, a union which allows you to grow on an inner level as well as an outer. This card can symbolise the beginning or deepening of a relationship, and also building and enjoying partnerships in a more general sense. You are likely to be feeling compassionate and empathetic towards others, able to appreciate their uniqueness and the gifts they bring to your life. The Two of Cups symbolises positive and helpful unions, the connections you make with others, especially one to one, which helps you to get to know yourself better. Meeting the other person as they really are, rather than as we want them to be, is really important with this card, otherwise you risk building relationships based on your own projections rather than a genuine connection.

## *THREE OF CUPS*

The Three of Cups traditionally symbolises friendships and social connections, feeling positive and enjoying life. Its a card of abundant emotions, celebrating with loved ones, and feeling content and happy. The gifts of joy and laughter bring just a much inner growth and change for us as do suffering and painful emotions, so this card asks you to make space in your life to feel and enjoy those positive emotions, and to take a light-hearted approach. On a deeper level, this card symbolises the emotional security which comes from knowing where you belong and feeling comfortable and able to be yourself. It's about finding your soul friends, the people who are family whether you are related to them by blood or not. The Three of Cups is a card of building and celebrating those connections and enjoying the deep emotional bond they bring.

## FOUR OF CUPS

When the Four of Cups appears, it indicates that you might be feeling stuck in a rut, perhaps somewhat self-absorbed or apathetic, unable to see the gifts life offers you. You may have a sense of dissatisfaction, perhaps feeling that something isn't quite right but not really knowing what to do about it. You may feel trapped in old emotional patterns, unable or unwilling to move out of them. The Four of Cups can indicate a necessary period of introspection, a time to get in touch with your feelings and process any past emotions which you no longer need and which may be holding you back. Past hurts can blind you to new opportunities, meaning that you hold yourself back in fear and remain in your comfort zone. Whilst it's understandable that you fear being hurt again, you also risk missing out on positive new connections.

## FIVE OF CUPS

The shifts and changes of the Fives, in the feeling realm of the Cups, can mean feeling loss or regret and needing to acknowledge painful emotions in order to begin the healing process. The Fives of Cups can indicate a time of grief or disappointment, of feeling let down or hurt by someone that we cared about, and needing to take the time to process the experience. It's important not to repress or ignore difficult feelings, or they have a tendency to reappear in a much more destructive form. On the other hand, this card also counsels against spending too much time wallowing in self-pity or blaming others for what has happened to you. Only you can make the choice to move on, and this card affirms that the time will come and that negative feelings do not define you.

## SIX OF CUPS

The traditional meanings for the Six of Cups include nostalgia, childhood, and innocence. You may find yourself thinking about the past, about the influence it had on your growth and the choices you made in life. This can be helpful, if you use your memories creatively, but can also lead to viewing life through rose-tinted spectacles. Sometimes the past is idealised and it's important to appreciate all the experiences, good and bad, which made you the person you are today. Attending to unfinished business is useful, as long as it doesn't hold back your current growth. On a deeper level, this card can symbolise getting in touch with our inner child, perhaps rediscovering y creativity or ability to play and finding new ways to express your true self. The Six of Cups invokes positive feelings of kindness and generosity, empathy and compassion for others.

## SEVEN OF CUPS

The seven of Cups is traditionally seen as a card of daydreaming and wishful thinking, of having so many options that you are unable to settle on any of them. The seven Cups in the image are often shown full of various items which may tempt us, such as jewels, fruits, the snake which symbolises regeneration or the laurel wreath which symbolises victory. When the Seven of Cups appears, you may be feeling that you want it all, or that you have no idea what you want. The Seven of Cups can symbolise illusions and an excess of imagination. This is a card of abundance, but it also indicates a need for discernment, for looking closely at each option and deciding whether it is superficial or meaningful, something that we truly want or something that is imposed on us by others. This discernment is necessary to bring the products of your imagination into tangible reality.

## EIGHT OF CUPS

As with all of the Eights, the Eight of Cups brings an urge to reestablish harmony, a need to get back in touch whatever is most meaningful in your life. This may mean taking some time for introspection, to decide what that is and how to change your life to accommodate it. This card is often the beginning of a journey of inner discovery, moving on from what you have built so far to seek higher wisdom and deeper understanding. This may mean giving up parts of your life to which you have become attached, to give up on goals or plans which are no longer fulfilling or inspiring. This may not be popular with those around you and may mean going against the expectations of friends, family or mainstream society. The Eight of Cups is therefore also a card of being true to yourself, even if it means making some painful decisions.

# NINE OF CUPS

The Nine of Cups is often known as the "wish card", as it symbolises emotional and physical satisfaction, of having your wishes and dreams fulfilled, and enjoying the results of your hard work. It's a card of enjoying the pleasures of the senses, which may mean connecting more meaningfully to your emotions, or may mean ignoring them, especially the challenging ones. There is a sense of complacency about this card, a smugness and self-satisfaction which suggests a disconnection from others. Most versions of this card show a solitary figure, suggesting someone who is unable or unwilling to share their success. Whilst is good to enjoy the results of your hard work and the happiness you have earned for yourself, enjoying it alone may not be satisfying for long. This card symbolises the rewards of generosity and shared abundance, the realisation that holding your happiness for yourself limits it, whereas sharing it with others increases it.

## TEN OF CUPS

The Ten of Cups brings a deep sense of emotional fulfilment and emotional security, an awareness of the abundance and blessings of life. Most of the images for this card show a happy family or couple, secure in their deep connection and love for each other. This card indicates a sense of belonging to family or tribe, an appreciation of the support of others and the willingness to support others yourself. The Ten of Cups is a card of inspiration, love and harmony, of dreams coming true through your own sustained efforts. It carries a sense of "coming home" in an emotional sense, of discovering where you belong and the people you belong with. Whereas the Nine of

Cups suggests outer satisfaction, the Ten of Cups brings inner satisfaction, not just material abundance but emotional abundance too. You are able to see beyond yourself and appreciate all the gifts life has brought you.

## *PAGE OF CUPS*

The Page of Cups is beginning a journey of acknowledging and revelling in his feelings, of understanding them and also simply feeling them, even allowing them to overwhelm him at times. He has a strong sense of imagination and a deep ability to love, although he may be quite naïve and innocent.

He can be sensitive, but is loyal and trustworthy, and not afraid to be vulnerable. When this Page appears, you may need to open up and take an emotional risk, to let others see and understand the real you. It may be time to recognise and begin the work of understanding hidden emotions and intense feelings. Whilst this is easy for positive feelings such as joy and love, it's also important not to ignore the challenging feelings. The journey for this Page is the quest to feel all of our emotions,

however difficult and to appreciate their gifts.


## KNIGHT OF CUPS

The Knight of Cups is a romantic daydreamer, sensitive and fond of poetry and flights of fancy. In some ways he is the Knight closest to the chivalry and divine inspiration of medieval knights, risking all for love or for an idealistic dream. He feels intensely and may come across a quite dramatic at times, unable to see beyond his overwhelming feelings and his need to express them. He is charismatic, the kind of person others are drawn to, but may also be given to illusion or even deception, of himself as well as others. Unlike the Wand and Sword Knights, his horse is usually shown standing still, as for him the action and movement take place on an inner level. His quest is one of the heart, the quest for true love or devotion and service to a higher being or ideal.

## QUEEN OF CUPS

Kind and tenderhearted towards others, this Queen is empathetic and strongly in touch with her psychic side and her powerful imagination. She is sensitive and feels intensely, but has the power to hold these feelings and also to share them with others to inspire or reassure them. As well as being good at connecting to her own feelings, she can encourage others to acknowledge and express their own feelings and is likely to be seen as a caring and compassionate figure. She is closely connected with her dreams and intuition and is often shown with at least one foot in the waters of the unconscious. She symbolises emotional integrity, nurturing others with her love and care. She is often artistic and creative, seeking ways of expressing her emotions tangibly and in ways others can understand. She may also have a deep connection to the spiritual side of life.

## KING OF CUPS

A wise guide and counsellor, the King of Cups has a deep understanding of the emotional self and a strong sense of empathy. He has worked hard to gain mastery of the emotional realm and may put his skills to use as a counsellor or adviser for others. As with all the Kings, he carries the authority of the suit and takes responsibility for the realm of feelings and imagination. He understands and accepts that emotions are complicated, and this can make him detached, by choice or otherwise. Unlike his Queen, he is generally depicted standing or sitting completely on land, by the side of the water rather than in it. He chooses to stay disconnected in order to be able to heal, teach and help others, without getting drawn in or personally involved. He is creative but may be more focused on creating frameworks for helping others than on expressing his personal creativity.

# THE SUIT OF PENTACLES

## ACE OF PENTACLES

The Ace of Pentacles brings a divine gift of abundance which increases your possibilities for material security. It represents a surge of personal power and energy which you can use to increase your material abundance and build a more solid foundation for your endeavours. It may indicate a new awareness of a growing skill or talent, or new opportunities to practise those skills and talents. When the Ace of Pentacles appears, it brings favourable conditions for manifesting ideas, for starting a business or a new professional or artistic project. Everything may seem to fall into place so that suddenly you have all the resources you need, or a burst of inspiration may remind of resources that are already available to you. This Ace brings the potential for building a greater sense of self-worth and a feeling of inner as well as outer security.

## TWO OF PENTACLES

The Two of Pentacles symbolises the ability to be flexible and to find ways to balance all the demands that life makes of you. Most of the images for this card show a figure holding a pentacle in each hand, juggling or balancing them. Whether it's your job and your personal life, your family and your work or simply two different, equally demanding, projects, you may be finding that you are struggling to balance these different areas of your life. In the first place, the Two of Pentacles often simply affirms that you are able to do this, that you are learning to be flexible and how best to use your energies. This card asks you to enjoy the process and to appreciate the gifts and challenges of all of the different demands on your time and energy. Each is there for a reason and has something to teach you.

## *THREE OF PENTACLES*

When the Three of Pentacles appears, you may find yourself working with others in a team or group, making your contribution and enjoying the support of others. This is a card of shared effort, of coming together to build something that is greater than the sum of its parts. It can also symbolise the need and ability to ground your creative visions in physical work, to take the steps you need to bring your dream into reality. The Three of Pentacles indicates our skills, our mastery of them and our ability to use them to achieve our own and shared goals. It asks us to use them well, planning our work and working to our highest ability. This is a card of integrity, dedication and commitment. The Three of Pentacles also symbolises taking satisfaction and pleasure in our work, our ability to create something from nothing.

## FOUR OF PENTACLES

The fixed structure of the Four, in combination with the earthy energy of the Pentacles, creates something lasting and solid, and the ability to structure and organise your life. However taken too far, this can mean getting stuck in a rut, and sticking to the familiar, staying in your comfort zone and avoiding growth. It can also symbolise possessiveness, the urge to hold on to what we have, to cling to material possessions as the only means of security. This can mean that you close yourself off from a more meaningful life or a sense of something outside of yourself, leading to a limited vision or a perceived lack of possibilities. The Four of Pentacles can symbolise shelter and protection, which everybody needs, but can also indicate hiding in that shelter as a way of avoiding life. This card asks you to open up, to share what you have and to re-connect with the world.

## FIVE OF PENTACLES

The Five of Pentacles traditionally indicates a time of feeling insecure or lacking in support, a time when you are more aware of what you lack than what you have. Most of the images for it are of isolation or being left out in the cold, lacking in shelter or resources. Like all of the Fives, the Five of Pentacles indicates a time of transition, changes which may initially be prompted by outer circumstances but which lead to inner growth. The Five of Pentacles can be said to illustrate the dangers of relying too much on the material for your security. This can leave you spiritually bereft and lacking a sense of meaning so that the motivation to move forward and do something productive is lost. When the Five of Pentacles appears, its time to learn the lessons of the dark night of the soul and accept the support that is offered.

## SIX OF PENTACLES

The Six of Pentacles symbolises the process of giving and receiving, the exchange of energy which sustains us and those around us. This is a card of inner and outer resources, and of giving and taking, of learning to share what we have. You may be the wealthy merchant who is able to be generous or the poorer relation who needs to accept help. Many people actually find the latter more difficult, preferring to stay in the cold isolation of the Five rather than accept the extra support that may be offered. Whichever position you are in, this card asks you to take a look at your attitudes and habits around giving and receiving. Do you give out of genuine concern for others, or to make yourself feel better? Perhaps you are concerned that any help you accept might come with conditions or expectations. The Six of Pentacles brings a chance to gain awareness of these dynamics.

## SEVEN OF PENTACLES

The Seven of Pentacles often indicates a process of shifting the balance of your life away from material concerns and towards something more meaningful, for example moving from a job which pays the bills to a vocation which is more fulfilling and allows you to be true to yourself. It can also indicate a time to pause and allow your harvest to develop, reassessing or evaluating your situation. This card suggests an enjoyment of the work for its own sake, rather than a focus on the end goal or what you have achieved so far. Looking at what you have achieved so far brings its own rewards though, and this card indicates that you are beginning to see the results of your hard work and to make a genuine difference in the world. The

Seven of Pentacles indicates that patience and determination are the recipe for success.

## EIGHT OF PENTACLES

The Eight of Pentacles symbolises sustained effort, the repeated practising of a skill or honing of a talent. When this card appears, you are more likely to be working for the joy of it rather than in expectation of reward, working to gain mastery of your craft for your own personal satisfaction. On one level, this card is simply about focusing on the task before you and doing your best, taking your time to do a good job. On a deeper level, it can be about finding your passion, the work or vocation which brings you the greatest fulfilment and which will become your life's work. Like the Seven, this card carries energies of patience, determination and persistence. The rewards take time, but that is part of what makes them worth having. This is a card of giving service, to your higher self as well as the greater good.

## NINE OF PENTACLES

The Nine of Pentacles brings the rewards of your own efforts and the sense of security which comes from having achieved your goals. This is a card of discipline, self-control and self-reliance, and of reaping the rewards of long application of those qualities. The images for this card usually show a solitary figure standing in a garden, which symbolises fruition and fulfilment. The Nine of Pentacles indicates a time when you can enjoy a sense of material security and the knowledge that you have achieved that for yourself, through your own hard work. This card symbolises wealth and abundance, success and satisfaction, all coming from a sense of dedication to purpose and a strong and clear focus. It can mean taking the time to enjoy what you have, feeling secure in your values and the comfort you have built for yourself.

## TEN OF PENTACLES

The Ten of Pentacles brings a sense of affluence and abundance, on a material but also at a deeper level. Rather than a solitary figure, most versions of this card show an extended family, perhaps several generations, indicating that this card can mean a legacy, the urge to pass on not just material security but also the wisdom and learning of a life well lived. As with the other Tens, this card indicates sharing the lessons of the suit with the community and passing on the lessons learned, in readiness for closing this cycle of growth and beginning a new one. The Ten of Pentacles symbolises the security of family and inheritance, and also the sense of belonging to something greater than ourselves. This card can indicate where your roots are, or where you choose to put them down, and also a connection to your ancestors and an awareness of how they have influenced your life, directly or indirectly.

# PAGE OF PENTACLES

The Page of Pentacles epitomizes lifelong learning, the idea that all of life has something to teach us, and also that learning is not just about the intellect. He is beginning a journey of learning from experience, through study but also through observation, experimentation and simply doing the work. When the Page of Pentacles appears, its time to start putting your ideas into practice, beginning with small steps and building your momentum. This Page is patient and determined, but also always busy, believing that its important for both mind and body to be well occupied. He seeks ways to make a tangible difference in the world and sees his learning as something to apply in a practical situation, rather than an abstract understanding. His work is to change outward experiences to inner understanding, and so sometimes he may appear self-absorbed.

## KNIGHT OF PENTACLES

The Knight of Pentacles embodies diligence and hard work, a reliable figure who is trustworthy and loyal. He symbolises structure and organisation, and also dedication and commitment. He takes responsibility and accepts his obligations without complaint, and is more likely to focus on fulfilling his duty than on a personal quest or individual project. Sometimes this Knight is seen as dull, staid or even rigid, as he represents the need for steady hard work, drawing on the traditions of the past rather than seeking innovation. However, he always gets the job done, fulfilling all of his goals and commitments. He takes a methodical approach and is always productive, preferring to work towards a specific purpose rather than for the sake of it. Sometimes he is seen as a farmer, working with nature and the seasons to ensure that all grows in its due time.

# QUEEN OF PENTACLES

This Queen is an earth mother figure who nourishes and nurtures, providing practical help and advice as well as emotional support. She is resourceful and trustworthy and inspires others to make the best use of their talents by making the best use of her own. She embodies the abundance of nature and the gifts of the earth, and in some ways can be seen as a more down to earth version of the Empress. Like the other Queens, she holds and transforms the energy of her suit, and then radiates it outwards, encouraging others to live by their values and in harmony with their environment. She embodies the truth that by living and working with integrity, we can find satisfaction in our work and that work in the material realm can be an important path to spiritual growth and personal integration.

## KING OF PENTACLES

The King of Pentacles is an enterprising person who has a natural head for business and is able to make the most of an opportunity. He is shrewd, good at planning and taking a long-term view, willing to work hard to maximise his growth over time. As the master of the earthly realm, this King symbolises the rewards of sustained effort and our achievements in the material world. He has material abundance and likes to enjoy it, but he doesn't lose sight of what is really important, valuing people and connections over possessions. He is a good leader, although he may tend towards a more traditional rather than an innovative approach, valuing the past and the lessons it can teach us. He has high standards and good judgement and expects others to maintain those just as well as he does.

# CHAPTER FOUR : HOW TO DO A TAROT READING

## TAROT SPREADS AND HOW THEY WORK

A tarot spread is a map, or layout, in which you place cards in specific positions. A spread can contain anything from one or two cards to the whole deck, but most spreads contain between three and twelve cards. The spread you choose will depend on the question you want to ask, and how detailed you would like the answer to be. A spread might be one or two cards first thing in the morning to give an overview of the energies of the day or a reading for a full year with one or more cards for each month.

When doing a tarot reading, whether for yourself or someone else, taking your time to set up your space is important, as it helps to shift your mood and open up your intuition. You may like to light some candles or incense, and lay the cards out on a nice cloth which is only used for tarot readings. All of these actions create a "ritual" around the cards, reminding us that doing a tarot reading as a meaningful and important experience. The little rituals we use as we begin a reading help to align our inner and outer realities and open us up to messages from the universe and from our higher self.

Most tarot readings start with a question, even if it's only a vague desire to know what is happening around you at the moment. Asking the right question can be key to a good tarot reading, and it's worth taking some time before you start the reading to word your question carefully. The tarot doesn't tend to answer closed questions or those with seeking yes / no answers very well. What do I need to know about my relationship with X? works better than Does X love me? or Is X the one for me? Its always best to focus the question, and therefore the reading, on the querent themselves, rather than a third party. If they are nor present, or even aware that the reading is happening, their energies do not come through so clearly. There is also a question of ethics here, as asking about a third party invades their privacy. Many tarot readers also prefer to avoid emotive questions regarding pregnancy, health or the law, and if a querent asks you about such matters it is perfectly acceptable and even advisable, to refer them to the relevant professional.

Once you have decided on your question, and the spread you want to use, the next step is to shuffle the cards. Everyone has their own way of doing this, and you'll discover yours as you gain experience. Many people like to "cut" the deck by splitting it into three piles and then re-stacking them in a different order. When you are satisfied that you have shuffled the deck sufficiently (as with so much of tarot reading, this is a matter for your intuition, and over time you'll come to know when its "enough"), lay the cards down one at a time in the order and positions given in the layout diagram.

When doing a reading, we consider the story the cards tell. Each card is interpreted individually, but also in the context of both its position in the reading and also the cards around it. Once you have laid out the cards, look at them all together. Are there any similarities or cards which link together? For example, there may be lots of Cups cards, several Major Arcana cards or no Major Arcana cards, or more than one card with the same number. By looking at the overview of the spread, we can get a sense of the general energies of the reading. Lots of Cups cards might mean a time of emotional changes or when the querent is ruled by their feelings. Lots of Major Arcana cards implies that this is an important question, even if it doesn't seem so on the surface, whereas no Major Arcana cards would suggest that this is an everyday concern, with a relatively straightforward solution or result. Looking at the colours in the cards can also give us valuable information. Are they all bright, all dark, or is there a contrast? If there are people in the cards, which direction are they looking in? Do they face each other or have their backs to each other? All of these visual clues awaken our intuition and help us to decide the meaning of the cards in the specific context of this reading and this question.

# THE THREE CARD SPREAD, WITH

## EXAMPLES

The three card spread is one of the most popular and has many variations. Three cards is a good balance between not overloading yourself or your querent with information, whilst still gaining enough insight to show you a way forward. Some of the most popular include:

- Past, present, future,
- Issue, action, outcome,
- Body, mind, spirit,
- Situation, opportunity, challenge.

The cards are usually laid out in a straight line, as shown above, but they may also be laid out in a triangular shape. Examples of two three card readings are given below.

This is a past, present, future reading, for the simple question "What do I need to know right now?"

The Tower is in the past position, the Ace of Cups in the present, and the Fool in the future. Two Major Arcana cards in a three card reading is a high percentage, so immediately we can see that although the querent is asking a very general question, she seems to be going through some important changes, and may be struggling to get a grasp on them. The Tower in the past position confirms this, suggesting that there may have been some drama for the querent in the last few months and that it may not have been something that she chose or was able to control. However, the Ace of Cups in the present position shows that even if those changes felt difficult at the time, the way has been cleared for a new beginning. It may not be clear yet what that will look like, but there is a flow of emotional energy and a connection to the powers of the imagination which brings a sense of possibility and potential. Again, this is confirmed by the Fool as the future card. This shows the querent embracing those new possibilities and moving out of her comfort zone to a brand new chapter of life. The structures of the Tower have broken down, bringing the querent the freedom to follow her bliss, perhaps to do something she has dreamed of or imagined (the Ace of Cups) but has never had the courage to do before. We can see this process by looking at the colours of the cards. The dark greys of the Tower can feel oppressive, but the Ace of Cups and the Fool are much lighter and clearer, reflecting the calmer energies around the querent as she moves away from the experience of the Tower.

The querent for this reading asked, "What do I need to know about my relationship?" The first card, the Two of Cups, shows the current Situation, the second, the Lovers, shows the Opportunity available to the querent, and the final card, the Empress, shows a potential Challenge the querent may face. Again, there are two Major Arcana cards, so this is likely to be an influential relationship for the querent, which brings growth and possibly some life changes. The Two of Cups in the Situation position shows that this may be quite a new relationship and that both parties are feeling a strong sense of a soul connection, an attraction with the potential to develop into something more. They are likely to be getting on well and discovering that they have lots in common. The positive potential of this card is reflected in the Lovers as the Opportunity card, showing that this relationship has the potential to develop into something more meaningful. Both of these cards together show that the relationship is likely to bring opportunities to grow and find fulfilment for both individuals. The Empress in the position of Challenge shows what may cause problems in the relationship, or at least what will need to be faced in order for the relationship to thrive. On a literal level, the Empress may imply that having children could become an issue for the couple, perhaps with one partner more positive about the idea than the other. On a deeper level, it may suggest that one partner will find themselves "mothering" the other, with that partner putting more emotional energy into the relationship than the other. It could also mean that the couple will become so engrossed in their passion and pleasure in being together, that they neglect their duties or responsibilities. If you are reading for yourself, you will have a sense of which of these layers of meaning is most relevant. If you are reading for someone else, asking them some gentle questions, without prying, can help you both to figure out the energies going on. With a spread like this which flags up a potential challenge, the querent then has some concrete information to take away. In this case, they may decide to get clear on their own feelings about having children before talking to their partner. They may decide to draw some boundaries around how much emotional energy they are investing in "looking after" their partner, or they may realise that they are the one being looked after and resolve to do the same for their partner. The important thing is that they have a sense of how they can use the information the tarot has given them.

# THE CELTIC CROSS

The Celtic Cross is perhaps the most well known of all tarot spreads. It contains ten cards, set out in a cross shape consisting of the first six cards, with the remaining four in a column at the side.

1.    Your current situation

2.    What is challenging or opposing you at
      present

These two cards together represent the current energies around the querent, summing up the situation. The second card is usually an opposing energy to the first. This doesn't necessarily mean that the first card is positive and the second more challenging. If the querent is currently going through a challenging time, the second card may offer a more positive input.

3.      Conscious mind / higher self

4.      Hidden or unconscious influences

The cards above and below the central cross show the querent's state of mind. The bottom card reflects what is hidden, but may unconsciously be the driver for the current situation. The top card can show what is on the querent's mind, what she is most conscious of at this time. It also gives a sense of the highest potential available.

5.   Past

6.   Immediate future

The two cards to the right and left of the central cross are the timeline so that the central line of the reading is past, present and future. The Future card here shows the immediate future, perhaps if no action is taken or changes are made.

7.   Your inner self

The first card of the outside column shows how the querent is feeling, how they see the situation and also see themselves, and how these affect the situation in question.

8.   External influences

This card reflects the environment or circumstances around the querent, and how these factors might affect the question.


9.     Hopes and fears


This card shows how the querent's attitudes or assumptions might affect the course of events.

## 10.   Final outcome

The final outcome brings all the other cards together, combining the influences of the whole reading to give a possible or likely outcome. As with any tarot reading, this outcome is not fixed, and if it causes concern to the querent its common to pull one or two more cards to seek clarity on why such an outcome may happen, or how to avoid it.

# A SAMPLE READING USING THE

# CELTIC CROSS

The reading illustrated, using the Tarot of Marseilles, is for a querent asking what she needs to know about her career at this time. There are only two Major Arcana cards, and neither of them is in the central cross, showing that any changes are likely to feel more like an evolution than a revolution. There are quite a few cards which fall late in the number sequence, such as Tens and Eights, and also two which come at the beginning, an Ace and a Two. This suggests that there may be a phase ending and a new chapter beginning for the querent.

1.    King of Wands

The King of Wands as her current situation shows that she is already well established in her career, confident in her knowledge and able to take the lead both to direct others and to keep her own focus.

2.    Two of Wands

The Two of Wands in the opposing position shows that she may be seeking something new, making the decision to step away from what she has been doing so far and seek a new challenge.

3.    Ten of Cups

The Ten of Cups is a card of emotional abundance, and in the position of Conscious mind / higher self is suggests that she is currently very aware of her emotions and how they are affecting her. It may be that she loves her job, or possibly that she finds it overwhelming in some way. On the other hand, this card could be an indication that what is on her mind is more focused on family and feelings, and she is ready to leave the high flying career behind.

4.      Eight of Cups

As the unconscious influence, the Eight of Cups reinforces the possibility that the querent is ready to move on in some way. When this card appears in a reading, it usually means that the querent is seeking something more meaningful, a move out of their comfort zone towards a more fulfilling path.

5.      Ten of Pentacles

The Ten is the end of the number cycle and generally indicates that we have reached a culmination point. It may suggest that the querent needs to be careful not to focus so much on the material that she neglects her Ten of Cups feelings. In this position, the Ten of Pentacles suggests that she has built up a good level of material security, and now she is ready for a new, perhaps more meaningful challenge.

6.    Ace of Swords

In the Future position, the Ace of Swords brings in a brand new energy and is the only Swords card in the reading. This might suggest that the querent has not focused too much on her intellect in her career so far, but that now she is ready for study or some new ideas.

7.    The Chariot

In the position of Self, the Chariot indicates that the querent knows what she wants, and what she needs to do to get it. It suggests that she is a person with lots of control and focus, who doesn't hold back when she has set her mind to something.

8.    Seven of Cups

In contrast to the Self position, the Seven of Cups as outside influences may suggest that other people see the querent as lacking in focus or following an unrealistic dream. It might also suggest that those around her are making suggestions about what she should do, whereas she already knows, as indicated by the Chariot in the previous position. The Seven of Cups here might also suggest that people keep trying to "tempt" the querent off her intended course by giving her other options.


9.    The Emperor

As her card of hopes and fears, the Emperor may suggest that the querent wants to take a more responsible role in her career, perhaps moving into management or leadership. This is backed up by the King of Wands in the centre position. On the other hand, she may feel blocked by somebody who is already in such a position, or perhaps be fearful of losing control.

10.    Page of Pentacles

The Page of Pentacles is in the position of the final outcome, and like the Ace of Swords in the Future position suggests studying, or at least following a new path. The Pages bring a sense of curiosity and fascination to whatever they do, and this card suggests that taking such an approach is what the querent needs to revitalise her career.

## NEXT STEPS IN YOUR TAROT

## JOURNEY

As well as doing tarot readings, there are many other ways to use the cards which you can explore as you get to know them. There are many books and online resources giving spreads for just about every question under the sun, and in time you may also want to start inventing your own spreads. Keeping a tarot journal is a very useful exercise. In it, you can note down your daily cards, and keep a record of readings done for yourself and others. Over time your journal can become a valuable resource. You will be able to see the patterns in the cards that appear for you, how their meaning applies to your life and how that may change over time.

A powerful way to work with the cards and build a strong personal connection with them is to meditate on them or use them for visualisation. If you've never done this before, it may take a little practice, but its definitely worth persevering. The easiest way to begin is simply to journey in your imagination into the image on the card. To do this, find a time and place when you won't be disturbed, and somewhere you can sit or lie down comfortably. You may like to light a candle to indicate to your higher self that this is a meaningful process. Take a few minutes to relax your body and your breathing, and then hold the card in front of you and gaze lightly at the image. After a few minutes, close your eyes and hold the image in your mind. Once you have it there clearly, you can step into the image, moving from a two-dimensional version to a three-dimensional version. Using your active imagination, travel around inside the image, perhaps talking to the figures there or simply exploring. When you have finished, step back out of the image and into your body, and note your experiences in your journal.

Getting to know the tarot cards can be the journey of a lifetime, and there will always be something new to learn. As with all the best things in life, the most important thing is to enjoy the journey!

# *FURTHER READING*

Thanks for purchasing Julia Steylon's comprehensive guide on Tarot Card Reading. We recommend you also get her book on Astrology and Horoscopes.

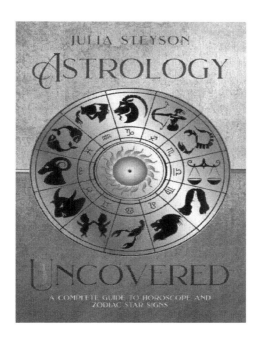

You can find it here:

https://www.amazon.com/Astrology-Uncovered-Guide-Horoscopes-Zodiac-ebook/dp/B07D6W64KZ

It is called: Astrology Uncovered: A Guide To Horoscopes And Zodiac Signs by Julia Steyson

And we also recommend you check out Julia Steyson's book on Wicca, Magic, Spells and Witchcraft. It will leave you spellbound!

It is called: Wicca Spell Book: The Ultimate Wiccan Book on Magic and Witches: A Guide to Witchcraft, Wicca and Magic in the New Age with a Divinity Code.

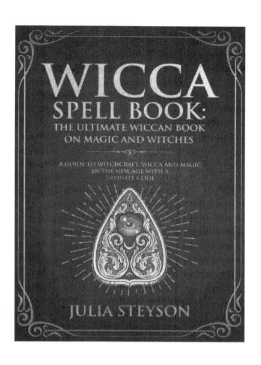

You can find it here:

https://www.amazon.com/Wicca-Spell-Book-Witchcraft-Divination-ebook/dp/B07GVLK9PZ

68276170R00107

Made in the USA
Columbia, SC
06 August 2019